CHRISTMAS IS COMING! 1985

CHRISTMAS IS COMING! 1985

Compiled and Edited by Linda Martin Stewart

Designed and Illustrated by David Morrison

Oxmoor House®

© 1985 by Oxmoor House, Inc.
Book Division of Southern Progress Corporation
P.O. Box 2463, Birmingham, Alabama 35201

Library of Congress Catalog Card Number: 84-063030

ISBN: 0-8487-0639-0

Manufactured in the United States of America
First Printing

Executive Editor: Candace Conard Bromberg
Production Manager: Jerry Higdon
Art Director: Bob Nance

Christmas Is Coming! 1985

Editor: Linda Martin Stewart
Project Coordinator: Fran Easterlin Dudley
Editorial Assistant: Lenda Wyatt
Copy Chief: Mary Jean Haddin
Photographers: Jim Bathie, Beth Maynor
Staff Artist: David Morrison

CONTENTS

A WORD TO PARENTS

As the editor of this book and as the mother of a child who marvels at every aspect of Christmas, I am doubly excited about *Christmas Is Coming! 1985*. I have always felt that the preparations for Christmas should be as special as the day itself, and as I grow older and Christmas comes each year clothed in even deeper meaning than the year before, I realize that one of the season's greatest joys is sharing in these preparations. This year my daughter and I will be doing just that, and as I think of all the fun we'll have, visions of pop-silly-sicles, candy cane reindeer, and Ducky Doodle blackboards dance through my head!

When you look through *Christmas Is Coming!*, you'll see that it's divided quite simply into two chapters. The first chapter, Children's Workshop, is a collection of Christmas crafts for children, including trimmings to fix—holiday decorations, cards, and wraps—and presents to make. The second chapter is entitled Parents' Workshop and is a collection of specially selected gifts for you to make for children.

Color photographs and illustrations, full-size patterns, and numbered instructions are included with each of the projects in Children's Workshop. As you glance over these projects, notice that suggestions (Before You Start) or words of caution (For Safety's Sake) sometimes precede the instructions. Also note that at the bottom of the first page of each project, there is a level rating of 1, 2, or 3,

with Level 1 indicating the quickest, easiest projects, and Level 3 the most difficult ones or those calling for adult supervision. The projects within Level 2 are easy but call for a certain skill, such as using a sewing needle, or for extra time and patience. Please understand that these ratings are intended only as guide. Believing that mother and father know best, I recommend that you look through these projects with your children and decide together which ones are suitable for them to make alone. By the way, the parents' projects are presented for ease and convenience in a fashion similar to the children's—with one or more color photographs, step-by-step instructions, and, when feasible, full-size patterns.

As I sit at my desk, collecting my closing thoughts, I glance up and my eyes meet those of the Sunday Bears. I look at the bears' sweet faces and can't help, for what must be the hundredth time, returning a smile. For months these bears have sat on my shelf, propped among books and stacks of papers, and for months these bears have brought me pleasure.

It's this same sort of pleasure—pure and simple—that I sense when I imagine getting ready for the Christmas season with *Christmas Is Coming!* at hand. My family is going to have so much fun. I'm certain that yours will, too!

Linda Martin Stewart

CHILDREN'S WORKSHOP
Happy Holiday Crafts

Rainbow Lollipops

Wouldn't the Sugarplum Fairy love these lively lollipops! Make them in all the colors of the rainbow and use lots of glitter for a sugary sparkle. Hang the lollipops on your Christmas tree or tie them onto presents.

You will need:
pencil
coffee can
colored poster paper
scissors
construction paper
white glue
waxed paper

clear glitter
lollipop sticks
clothespins
straight pin
fishing line
ribbon

4   *Level 1*

1. On the poster paper, draw around the coffee can to make two circles for the sides of the lollipop. Cut out the circles.

2. Cut decorations for the lollipops from construction paper or more poster paper. Glue the decorations onto one side of each of the two lollipop circles. Wrap the circles in waxed paper and put them under a book until the glue is dry.

3. Spread the decorated sides of the two circles with a little bit of glue and sprinkle them with glitter. Let the glue dry. Shake off the glitter that didn't stick.

4. Spread the plain side of one circle with lots of glue. Place the lollipop stick on the gluey circle. Press the other circle on top. Put clothespins around the edges of the circles to hold them together until the glue is dry.

5. Use a straight pin to make a hole in the top of the lollipop. Push a piece of fishing line through the hole and knot the ends for a hanger. Tie a ribbon around the lollipop stick to make a pretty bow.

Just Ducky!

There's nothing daffy about these ducks! Dressed for the holidays in their best top hats, they'll make dandy decorations for your Christmas tree.

You will need:
tracing paper
pencil
scissors
blue, white, and yellow felt
2 small white powder puffs
white glue
sequins
rickrack
scrap of fabric (for the scarf)
ribbon

1. Trace the patterns for the duck's hat, tail, bill, and foot on tracing paper. Cut out the patterns. Draw around the hat on blue felt, the tail on white felt, and the bill and foot on yellow felt. Cut out the felt pieces.

2. Glue the edge of one powder puff over the edge of the other powder puff to make the duck's head and body. Let the glue dry.

3. Glue the bill, foot, and tail to the underside of the duck.

4. On the front of the duck, glue a sequin for the eye. Glue rickrack on the hat and then glue sequins on the rickrack. Glue the hat onto the duck's head.

5. Cut a strip from the scrap of fabric for the scarf. Tie it around the duck's neck. Glue the scarf to keep it in place.

6. For a hanger, glue the ends of the ribbon to the back of the hat.

Hat

Tail

Bill

Foot

Snappy Soapbox Shopping Bags

If you can wrap a present, you can make soapbox shopping bags. Tuck candy or little surprises inside the bags and hang them on the tree.

You will need:
empty soapbox (the kind that holds a bar of soap)
pencil
scissors
wrapping paper in Christmas colors
cellophane tape
ribbon, tinsel cord, or string
tissue paper
stickers

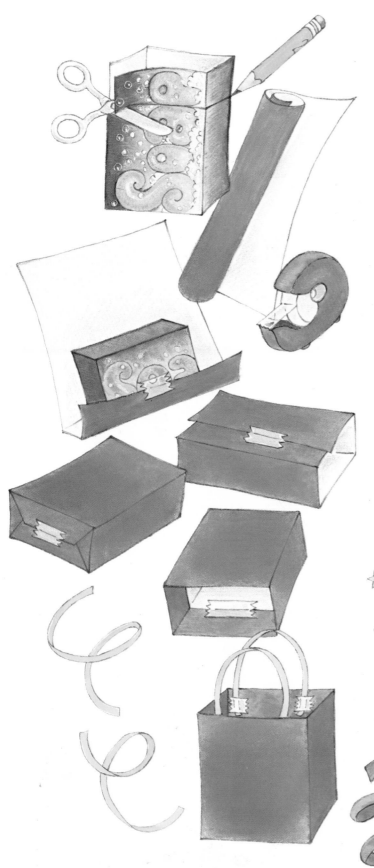

1. Decide how tall you want your shopping bag to be and cut the box to that height.

2. Cut a piece of wrapping paper that is big enough to wrap the box. Put the box in the middle of the paper. Wrap all but the open end of the box just as you would wrap a present. At the open end of the box, fold the ends of the wrapping paper to the inside of the box and tape them.

3. To make the shopping bag handles, cut two pieces of ribbon, tinsel cord, or string. Tape them to the inside of the box.

4. Cut a small piece of tissue paper and stuff it in the shopping bag. Decorate the bag with stickers, if you like. Fill the bag with goodies.

Candy Cane Reindeer

These candy cane reindeer are so easy to make that you won't need a lick of help! Make a boxful of these famous fellows. Give them for presents or party favors, or hang them on your tree.

You will need:
candy cane
2 chenille stems
scissors
white glue
2 plastic wiggly-eyes
red pom-pom
ribbon
jingle bell
fishing line

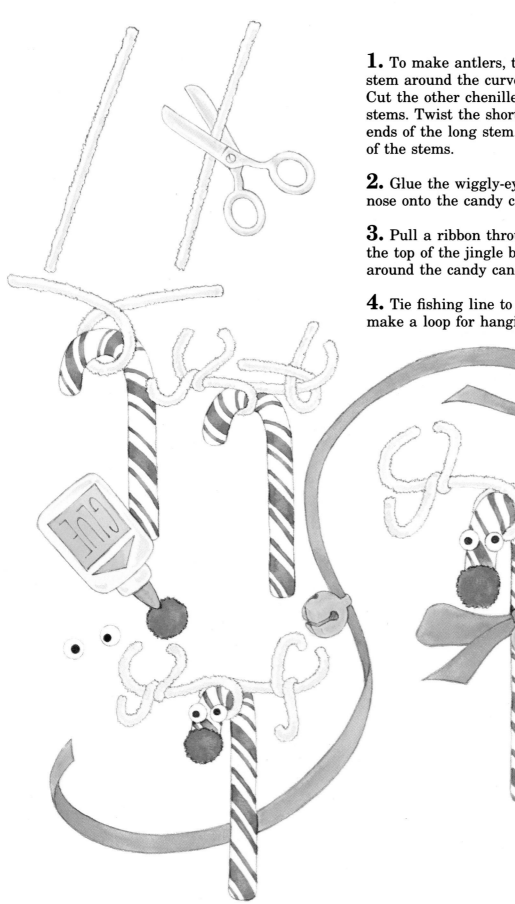

1. To make antlers, twist one chenille stem around the curve in the candy cane. Cut the other chenille stem into two short stems. Twist the short stems around the ends of the long stem. Turn up the ends of the stems.

2. Glue the wiggly-eyes and the pom-pom nose onto the candy cane.

3. Pull a ribbon through the opening at the top of the jingle bell. Tie the ribbon around the candy cane to make a bow.

4. Tie fishing line to the candy cane to make a loop for hanging.

11

Take-the-Cake Cupcakes

Little brothers and sisters can share in the fun of "cooking up" a batch of these colorful cupcakes. How yummy they look! But don't be fooled. These cakes aren't for eating—they're for trimming the tree!

For safety's sake: You'll need to ask your mom to help you use the electric mixer and to cut the plastic foam balls in half.

Making the Royal Icing

You will need:
3 large egg whites (no yolks!)
½ teaspoon cream of tartar
1 (16-ounce) package powdered sugar, sifted
large mixing bowl
spatula
electric mixer
4 small bowls
4 spoons
red, green, and yellow food coloring
plastic wrap

1. Put the egg whites in a large mixing bowl. (Warm egg whites make a bigger batch of icing than cold ones. So, if they're cold, let the egg whites sit out awhile before you beat them.)

2. Add the cream of tartar. Turn the electric mixer to medium speed and beat the egg whites until they are frothy.

3. Add some of the powdered sugar to the egg whites. Mix the sugar and egg whites on medium speed. Add more sugar and mix again. Keep adding sugar and mixing until you have added all of the sugar.

4. Beat the sugar and egg whites on medium speed until they form icing. This will take about five minutes.

5. Divide the icing into the four small bowls. Using a different spoon for each color, stir food coloring into the icing in three of the bowls. Leave one bowl of icing white. Cover the bowls with plastic wrap so that the icing will stay soft. (If it's okay with your mom, you can eat any icing that is left in the mixing bowl.)

Icing the Cupcakes

You will need (for six cupcakes):
6 silver foil baking cups
muffin tin
spoon
Royal Icing (pink, green, yellow, and
  white)
6 paper napkins (lunch size)
6 paper clips
3 (2½″) plastic foam balls
knife for icing the cupcakes
little candies
narrow ribbon

1. Put the foil baking cups into the muffin tin.

2. Place a spoonful of icing in a baking cup. Unfold a paper napkin, crumple it, and place it on top of the icing. Spread a spoonful of icing on top of the napkin.

3. Ask your mom to cut the foam balls in half. Push a paper clip a little more than halfway into the top of one of the half-balls. Hold the half-ball by the paper clip and spread the top with icing. Place the half-ball on top of the crumpled napkin.

4. Decorate the cupcake with little candies while the icing is still soft. If you use colored sugar crystals, sprinkle them on the cupcake lightly at first to make sure that the color does not run.

5. Make the rest of the cupcakes, one at a time. Leave the cupcakes in the muffin tin until the icing is hard.

6. Cut twelve pieces of ribbon. Pull one ribbon through each paper clip and knot the ends to make a hanger. Pull another ribbon through each paper clip and tie a bow.

Pop-Silly-Sicles

Decorate your Christmas tree with these frosty favorites—and hope that no one tries to take a bite!

You will need:

newspaper
scissors
ruler
pencil
paper clips
craft sticks
masking tape
measuring spoons

colored tissue paper
white glue
water
foil pie pan
clear glitter
ribbon

Level 2

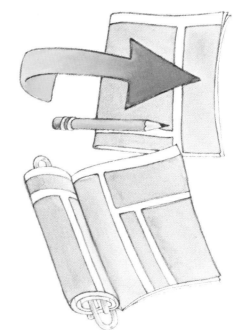

1. Take two double pages from a newspaper that your mom and dad have already read. Cut the double pages apart on the line where they have been folded so that you have four single pages.

2. Stack the pages one on top of the other. Measure and mark lines 4″ from the top and 3″ from one side of the stacked papers. Cut along the lines and then throw away the strips.

3. Fold the stacked papers in half, bringing the top edge of the papers to the bottom edge of the papers. Fold the papers in half again, the same way, bringing the top to the bottom.

4. Fold the papers in half a third time, but this time bring the left side of the papers to the right side of the papers. Rub up and down along the fold line with the side of your pencil to make a crease. This crease will be between the two sides of the pop-silly-sicle.

5. Open the paper. Roll one side of the paper toward the crease in the middle. Use paper clips to hold the roll in place. Roll the other side and clip the roll.

6. Run a long piece of masking tape down the crease between the two rolls, around the bottom, and up the back between the two rolls. Take off the paper clips. To make a hanger, tape one of the paper clips to the top of one of the rolls. Cover the rolls with strips of masking tape. In the bottom of each roll, make a cut in the tape and push a craft stick through the cut.

7. Cut the tissue paper into strips. Mix three tablespoons of glue with three tablespoons of water in the pie pan.

8. Dip the strips of tissue paper into the glue mixture, one at a time, and then smooth them onto the pop-silly-sicle. When you have covered up all of the tape, sprinkle glitter over the pop-silly-sicle. Let it dry overnight.

9. To hang the pop-silly-sicle, pull a ribbon through the paper clip and knot the ends.

These Are Tops!

If you would like to make these ruffly ornaments, you'll need to drink a lot of juice! Can you guess the reason why?

Before you start: Ask your mom to teach you how to sew a running stitch and pull the thread to make a ruffle, so you can ruffle the ribbon to glue on the lid. If you'd rather not sew, ask your mom to buy some narrow, pregathered eyelet. Lace bright ribbon through the eyelet and then glue the lid to it.

You will need (for each ornament):
pencil
tracing paper
scissors
peel-off lid from (12-ounce) frozen juice
 can
piece of corrugated cardboard
cellophane tape
hammer and nail (long, skinny one with a
 head)
needle and thread
24 inches (1¼″-wide) cut-edge or taffeta
 ribbon
tomato paste can
white glue
narrow ribbon

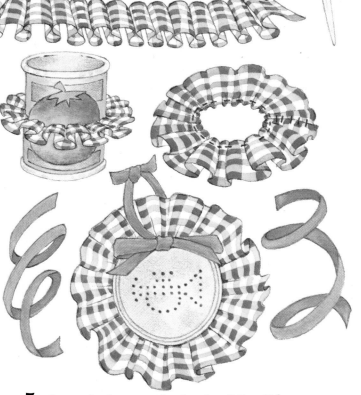

1. On tracing paper, trace the dots for the horn, bell, or drum. Then trace the circle around the dots. Cut out the paper circle.

2. Place the lid on the corrugated cardboard. Tape the paper circle on top of the lid. Using the hammer and nail, make a hole in the lid through each dot that is on the paper. Take the paper circle off the lid. Make one hole in the top of the lid for the ribbon hanger.

3. Sew a running stitch along the 24″ ribbon, about ¼″ from the edge. Pull the thread and gather the ribbon to make a ruffle. Bring the ends of the ruffle together to make a circle.

4. Put the tomato paste can in the middle of the ruffle. Gently push the gathers and pull the thread to make the ruffle fit tightly around the can. Keep your thumb on the ends of the ruffle and take out the can. Place one end of the ruffle on top of the other and sew the ends together.

5. Spread glue on the back of the lid, just around the edges. Press the lid on top of the ruffle. Place a heavy book on the lid and leave it until the glue is dry.

6. Cut two pieces of narrow ribbon. Pull one ribbon through the hole in the top of the lid and knot the ends to make a hanger. Tie the other ribbon into a bow around the hanger.

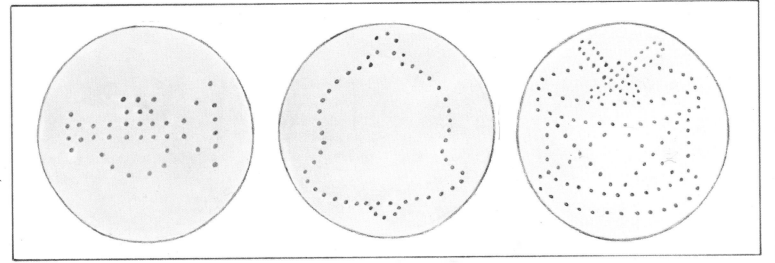

A "Beary" Nice Candle Ring

These chubby brown bears seem right at home sitting around a big red candle atop a table. Add applesauce to cinnamon for a dough to make the little bears. Mmm . . . they smell so good!

You will need:
1 (3¾ ounce) can ground cinnamon
large bowl
mixing spoon
applesauce
waxed paper
pencil
tiny red satin bows
white glue
6″ circle of heavy cardboard
big red candle
greenery

1. Pour the can of cinnamon into the large bowl. Add a spoonful of applesauce and stir. Keep adding applesauce, a little at a time, and stirring until you've made a stiff dough. Be careful not to add too much applesauce.

2. Place a piece of waxed paper on the table. Roll a ball of dough about the size of a big jawbreaker for the bear's body. Roll a ball that is a little smaller for the bear's head. Roll five balls that are half as big as the ball for the head. Use four of these balls for the paws. Divide the last ball in half and roll two tiny balls for ears.

3. Make little holes in the ears with the point of a pencil and stick the ears on the bear's head. Poke holes for the eyes. Stick the head, and then the paws, on the bear's body. To make the bear sturdier, gently pinch together the edges of all of the balls. Then smooth the bear.

4. Make about ten bears. When you have finished, set the bears aside on waxed paper and let them dry—untouched!—for several days. Allow the bears to dry thoroughly, or they will tend to have accidents, such as losing paws, ears, and heads. Do not try to dry the bears in the oven.

5. When the bears are dry, glue the red bows onto their necks. Let the glue dry.

6. Set the bears around the edge of the cardboard circle, with their paws touching. Because cinnamon bears are made in all sizes, just like people, you may need to add a bear or take one out in order for them to fit. When you have the right number, glue the bears onto the cardboard circle. Let the glue dry thoroughly so that the bears will be sure to keep their seats.

7. Put a big red Christmas candle in the center of the circle. Tuck some greenery among the bears, and you have a "beary" nice candle ring!

Away in a Manger

Setting up a scene that looks like the stable where Jesus was born is a nice way to celebrate Christmas. You can make Mary and Joseph, Baby Jesus, the shepherds and kings, an angel, and the animals for the scene, which is called a crèche, from felt. Glue the felt figures onto blocks of wood. Place them on a mantel or a table or under the Christmas tree.

Before you start: Ask your mom or dad to cut six 7½"-long blocks, four 6"-long blocks, and three 4"-long blocks from a 2" x 4" x 8' pine stud. After the blocks are cut, rub sandpaper on the ends to make them smooth.

You will need:
12 envelopes
pencil
tracing paper
scissors
different colors of felt
13 blocks of wood
white glue
ribbon, braid, and rickrack
sequins
felt-tip marker

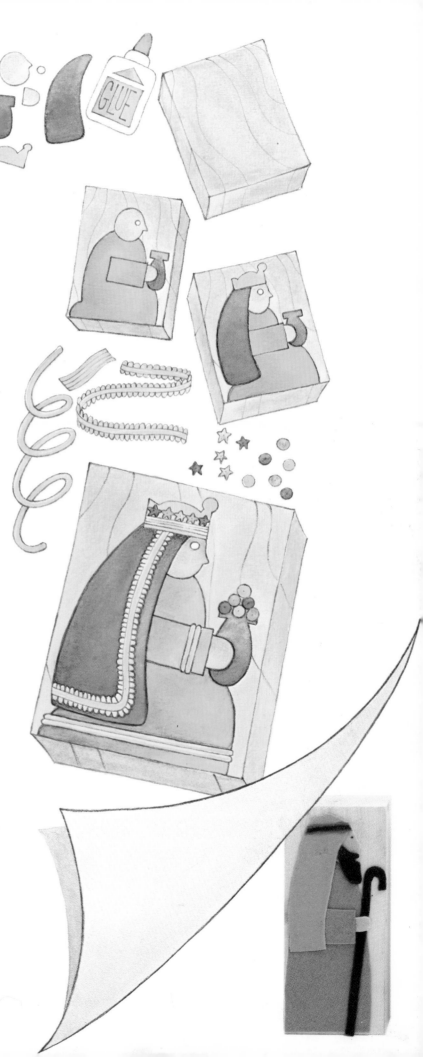

1. Look at the picture of the crèche figures and read the labels on the pattern pieces to see which pattern pieces go with each figure. Notice that sometimes you use the same pattern pieces to make different figures.

2. Label the envelopes with the names of the different figures. Trace the pattern pieces for each figure onto tracing paper. Cut out the pattern pieces. Put them in the envelope that is labeled with the figure's name.

3. Working on one figure at a time, draw around the pattern pieces on different colors of felt. Notice that you will need to turn over the pattern pieces for Mary and the Second Shepherd before you draw around them so that the figures will face in different directions.

4. Cut out the felt pieces for one figure at a time. As you finish cutting out each figure, put the felt pieces in place on a block that is the right size. (Put Baby Jesus and the Lambs on the 4″ blocks; put Mary, the Third King, the Donkey, and the Cow on the 6″ blocks; and put Joseph, the Angel, the First King, the Second King, the First Shepherd, and the Second Shepherd on the 7½″ blocks.)

5. When you have finished cutting out the pieces for the figures and have put them in place, glue them onto the blocks.

6. Glue bits of ribbon, braid, and rickrack onto the figures for trim. Glue sequins on the kings. Cut "spots" from felt and glue them on the cow. Make features for the figures' faces with the felt-tip marker or tiny pieces of felt.

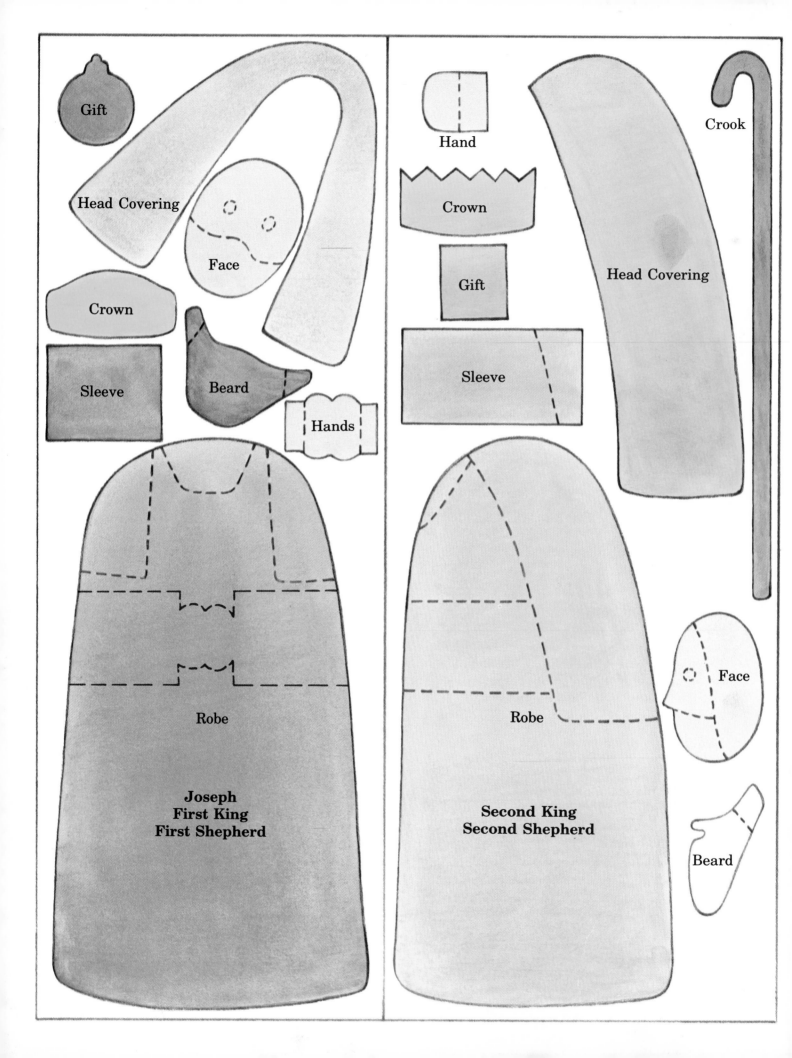

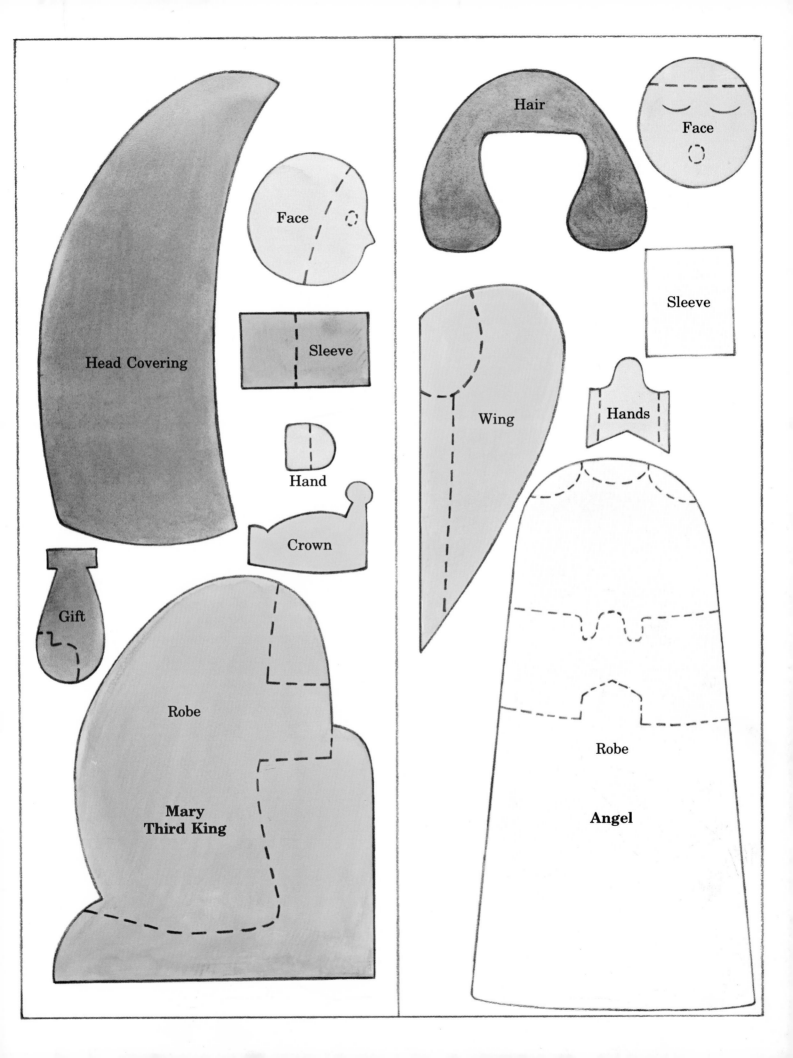

Face

Head Covering

Sleeve

Hand

Crown

Gift

Robe

**Mary
Third King**

Hair

Face

Sleeve

Wing

Hands

Robe

Angel

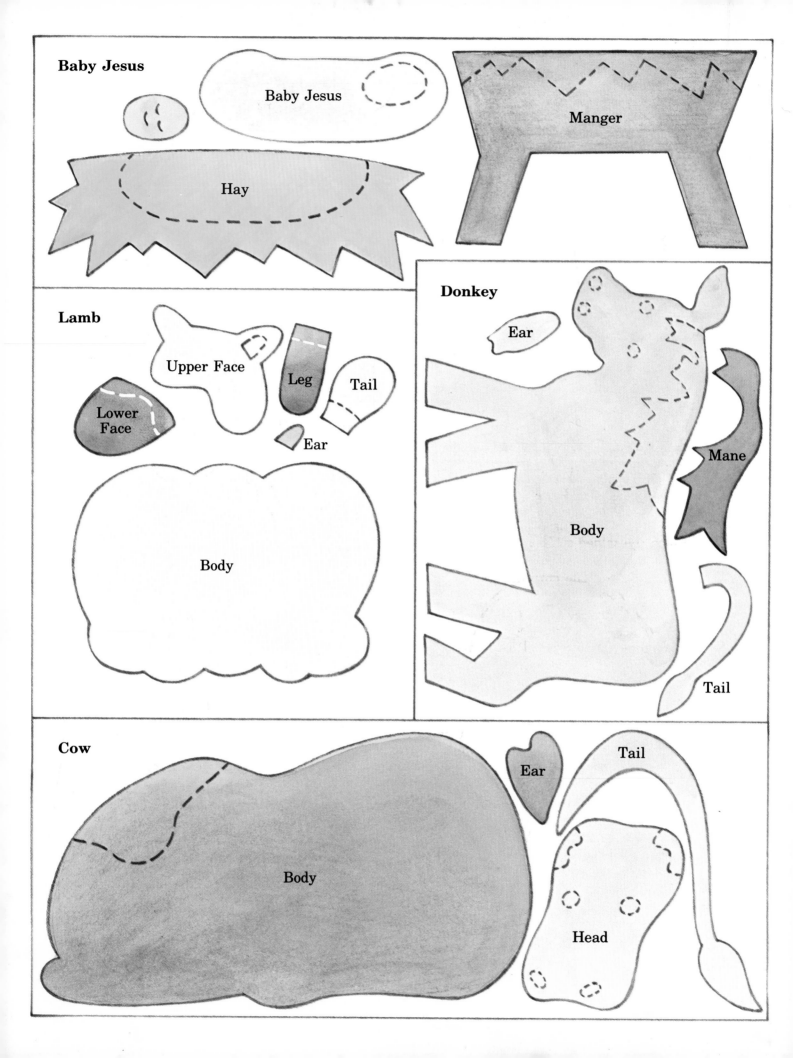

Baby Jesus

Baby Jesus

Manger

Hay

Lamb

Upper Face

Leg

Tail

Lower Face

Ear

Body

Donkey

Ear

Mane

Body

Tail

Cow

Body

Ear

Tail

Head

Here We Go Loop-De-Loop!

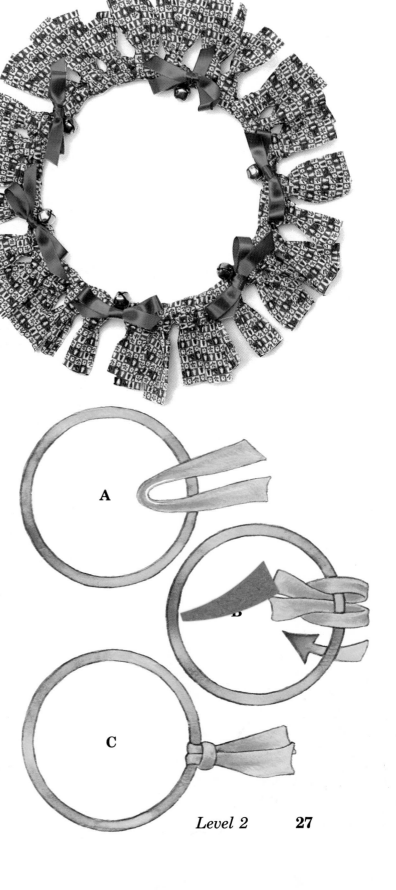

Making this merry-looking wreath is a cinch! Knot loops of gaily colored ribbon around a hoop. Then fasten jingle bells with satin bows to add a little shine.

You will need:
ruler
9⅔ yards (1⅜″-wide) cut-edge ribbon
scissors
11″ macrame hoop
3 yards of satin ribbon
jingle bells

1. Cut the cut-edge ribbon into pieces that are about 12″ long.

2. Fold one ribbon in half to make a loop. Place the folded ribbon on top of the hoop, with the loop toward the inside. (Drawing A.) Place the cut ends of the ribbon together and bring them behind the hoop and through the loop in the ribbon. (Drawing B.) Place one ribbon end on top of the other and pull both ends to tighten the knot. (Drawing C.)

3. Loop and knot each ribbon in the same way, side by side, all the way around the hoop. When you have finished, pull apart the ends of the ribbon to make the wreath look fluffier.

4. Cut the satin ribbon into pieces that are about 18″ long. String a jingle bell in the middle of each ribbon. Tie one ribbon to the hoop, between two knotted loops, and make a bow. Skip about five loops and tie another ribbon bow. Going around the wreath, tie all of the ribbons into bows.

Sweet Street

Ask your mom if you can invite a friend to make these houses with you. Building graham cracker houses is twice as easy—and twice the fun!—if you have four hands instead of two.

Before you start: Ask your mom to use the recipe on page 12 to make the Royal Icing, but leave the icing white—do not add the food coloring.

You will need:
graham cracker squares
waxed paper
bowl of Royal Icing (white)
knife for spreading the icing
index card
scissors
little candies
miniature marshmallows
tiny twigs
black felt-tip marker
green paste food coloring
small bowl
spoon
sugar cones
plastic snowflakes (the kind that you buy in a bag)

1. To make the walls of each house, lay one graham cracker on a sheet of waxed paper. Put icing around the edges of four other graham crackers. Stand them around the one that is on the waxed paper. Let the icing dry.

2. Use two graham crackers and icing to make a roof. Place it on top of the graham cracker walls.

3. From an index card, cut two triangles that are big enough to cover the holes at either end of the house. Spread icing on the triangles and then place them over the holes.

4. Cut windows and doors from graham crackers and "glue" them with icing onto the house. Decorate the house with more icing and a lot of little candies.

5. Make more houses. Set all of the houses aside to dry.

6. Put a bit of white icing between two miniature marshmallows to make the snowman. Use tiny round candies for earmuffs and tiny twigs for arms. Draw two dots for eyes with the black marker.

7. To make the sugar cone Christmas trees, place some of the white icing in a small bowl. Mix green paste food coloring with the icing. Spread the icing on the outside of the sugar cones. Shake candy sprinkles over the icing. Let the icing dry.

8. Set the houses, the snowman, and the trees on a table or mantel. Make candy walkways. Then sprinkle the snow.

Perky Paper Reindeer Wrap

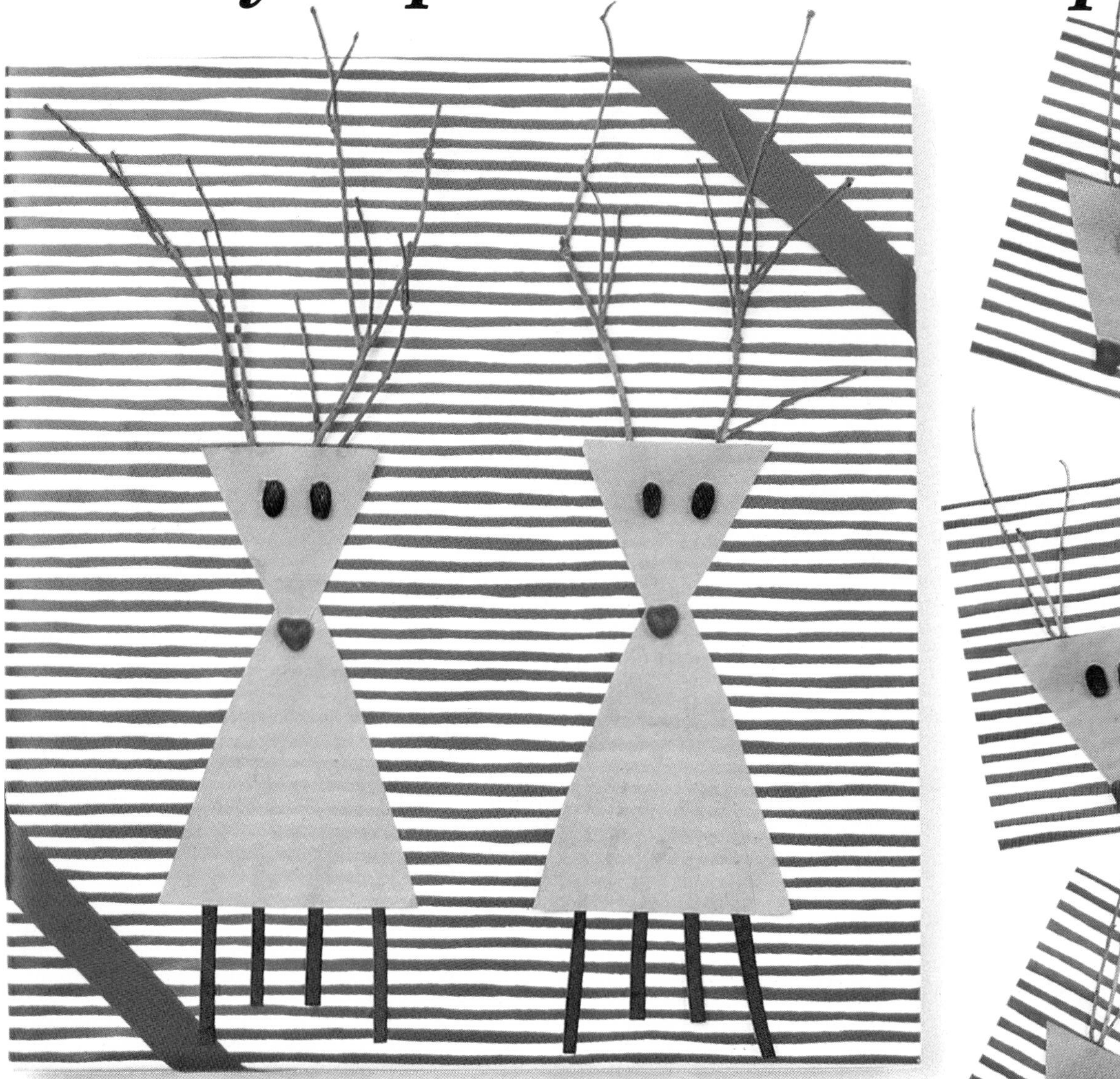

These perky paper reindeer are lots of fun and very easy to make. Glue the reindeer on top of a present. "No peeking inside!" they seem to say.

You will need:
pencil
tracing paper
scissors
brown mailing paper
black construction paper
wrapped present
white glue
twigs
seeds
red candy hearts
wrapping paper to match present (for the gift card)

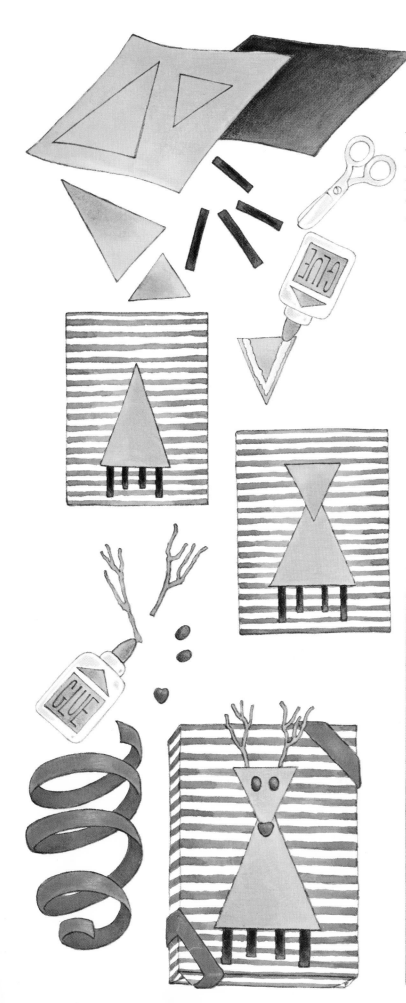

1. Trace the little triangle and the big triangle on tracing paper. Cut out the triangles. Draw around them on brown mailing paper to make the reindeer's head and body. Cut out the triangles. Then cut four strips from black construction paper for the reindeer's legs.

2. Glue the black strips on top of a wrapped present. Glue the big triangle over the top of the strips. Turn the little triangle upside down. Spread glue along the sides of it, but not along the top. Place the point of the little triangle over the point of the big triangle.

3. For antlers, put glue on the ends of the twigs and slide them under the top of the little triangle. Glue on seeds for eyes and a candy heart for the little red nose.

4. To make a gift card, cut a small piece of wrapping paper and fold it in half. Cut out a very little reindeer—or just a dear little reindeer face—and glue it onto the card. Add antlers, eyes, and a nose.

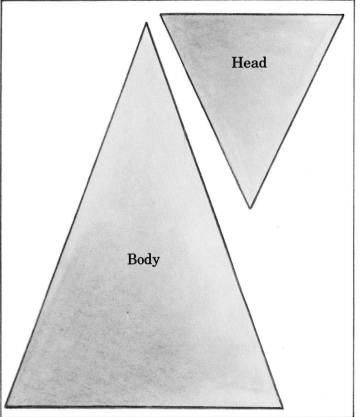

Head

Body

Tidings from Teddy

Dab-a-dab-a-do! That's how you paint this fuzzy brown bear. Dab Teddy on a tag or card. He's very good at bearing gifts and happy holiday wishes!

You will need:
pencil
piece of clear plastic (the thick kind that you buy at a craft store)
scissors
masking tape
construction paper
newspaper
small foil pie pan
brown, yellow, and white tempera paint
paintbrush with stiff bristles
black felt-tip marker
white glue
ribbon
jingle bells

1. Trace the pattern for Teddy on the piece of clear plastic. To make a stencil, cut into one side of the plastic and cut around the bear. Tape the cut to hold the edges together. (You will not need the bear that you cut out. The stencil is the piece of plastic with the bear-shaped hole.)

2. Make a card by folding or cutting construction paper. Place the card on a piece of newspaper. Place the stencil on top of the card. Put little pieces of tape around the edges of the stencil to hold it in place.

3. Put some brown paint in the pie pan. Add a little white and a little yellow paint and mix it all together to make a nice, warm brown for painting the bear.

4. Dip the paintbrush into the paint. Move the brush back and forth across a paper towel to remove most of the paint. Then dab the brush up and down inside the cutout in the stencil. Keep dabbing until you've made a bear. Take the stencil off the card.

5. Glue pieces of ribbon across the top and bottom of the card or around the edges of the card. Use the black marker to give Teddy two eyes, a nose, and a mouth. Glue a bright bow onto the bear's neck and, if you like, glue jingle bells beneath the bow.

Paper Sack House Wrap

Make a house for a Christmas wrap—with a grocery sack, paper cutouts, ribbon, and glue! These sack houses are neat for wrapping presents that are lumpy or bumpy or too big for a box. They are great for wrapping goodies like popcorn, too!

You will need:
large grocery sack
poster paper
ruler
pencil
scissors
pinking shears
hole punch
ribbon
scraps of wrapping paper
white glue
felt-tip marker

1. Place a present inside the grocery sack. (If the present is something to eat, first put it in a plastic bag.) Fold down the top of the sack.

2. Cut a piece of poster paper that is about 13″ x 19″. Fold the paper in half and make a crease. Use pinking shears to make zigzags along the edges of the paper. Place the folded paper over the top of the sack to make the roof.

3. Glue a small piece of poster paper on top of a bigger piece of wrapping paper to make a gift card. Punch a hole in the card. Punch two holes side by side through the middle of the roof and the top of the sack. String a ribbon through the holes in the roof, sack, and gift card. Tie the ribbon into a big, pretty bow.

4. Cut a door, a window, shutters, and a Christmas tree from wrapping paper. Glue the cutouts onto the sack. Draw panes on the window with the felt-tip marker. To make circles for Christmas balls, punch holes in red wrapping paper. Glue the circles onto the tree.

"Sew-Easy" Christmas Cards

Katie

MERRY CHRISTMAS! FROM: TOMMY

Merry Christmas To:

Mary

Love, Lisa

Use bright, fluffy yarn to stitch these colorful cards. Send them to faraway friends to wish them a Merry Christmas!

You will need:
tracing paper
pencil
scissors
white construction paper
felt-tip markers
plastic needle for sewing with yarn
white glue

For the Candy Cane Card: 1⅓ yards of white yarn, 8 inches of green yarn

For the Stocking Card: 1⅓ yards of red yarn

For the Christmas Tree Card: 1⅓ yards of green yarn, star sticker

Candy Cane Card

1. Trace and cut out the candy cane. Cut a card from construction paper. With a red marker, draw around the candy cane on the card. Color the candy cane red.

2. Thread the needle with the white yarn and pull the yarn so that the ends are even. Tie the ends together in a knot.

3. To sew the stripes, start from the back of the card at the bottom of the candy cane. Pull the needle UP through hole 1 and push the needle DOWN through hole 2. Sew stripes, in this way, all the way around the candy cane. When you have finished, cut the yarn and glue the ends to the back of the card.

4. Tie a bow with the green yarn and glue it onto the candy cane. Write "Merry Christmas" and then your name—in your fanciest letters!

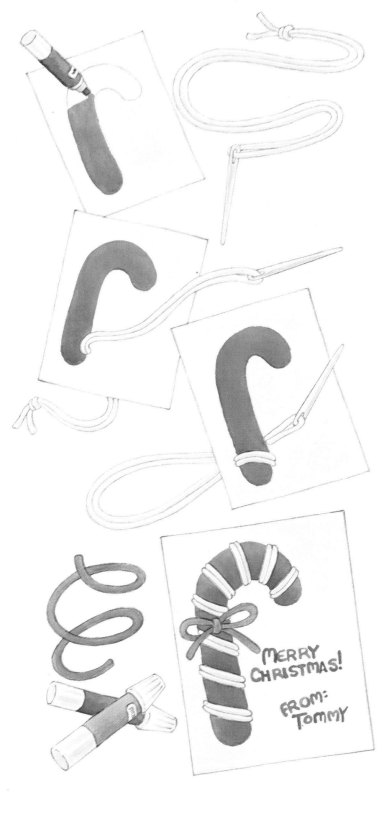

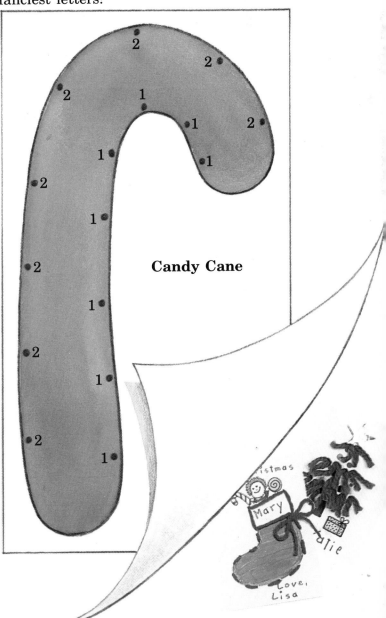

Candy Cane

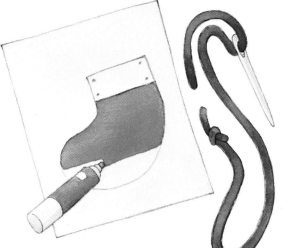

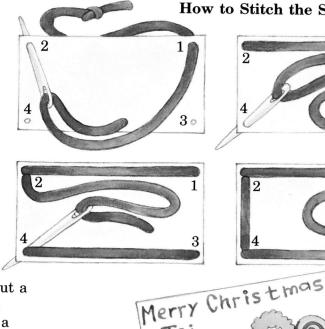

Stocking Card

1. Trace and cut out the stocking. Cut a card from construction paper. On the card, draw around the stocking with a green marker. Color the bottom of the stocking green, but leave the top, where you will write a name, white.

2. Thread the needle with the red yarn. Pull the yarn so that one end is longer. Tie a knot in the long end.

3. Look at the drawing to see how to stitch the top of the stocking and to find the numbers for the holes. Start from the back of the card. Pull the needle UP through hole 1, DOWN through hole 2, UP through 3, and DOWN through 4. Then pull the needle UP through 2, DOWN through 4, UP through 1, and DOWN through 3. (Whew . . . good work!) Cut the yarn and glue the end to the back of the card.

4. Make stitches around the bottom of the stocking. (You may want to poke holes for the stitches first.) When you have finished, cut the yarn and glue the end to the back of the card.

5. Tie a bow with the leftover yarn and glue it onto the stocking. Write the name of the friend for whom you are making the card across the top of the stocking. Then draw pictures of presents that your friend would like Santa to bring. Write a message and sign your name.

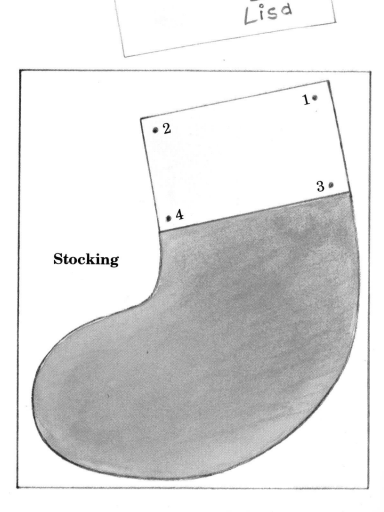

Stocking

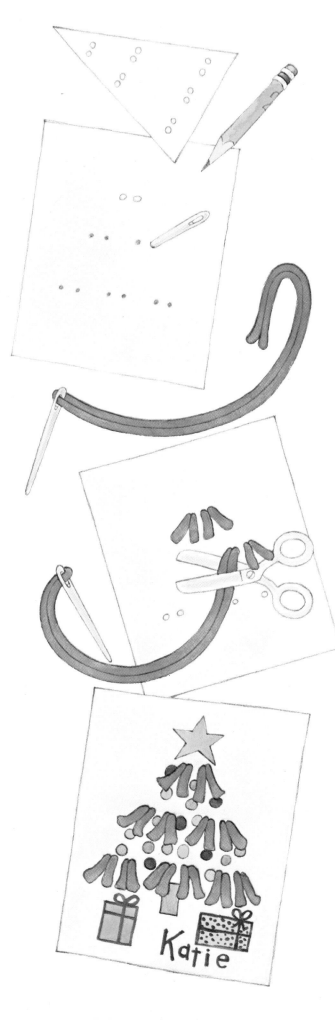

Christmas Tree Card

1. Trace the tree pattern and the dots onto tracing paper. Cut out the tree. Poke holes in the dots with the yarn needle.

2. Cut a card from construction paper. Place the tree on top of the card. Then poke holes in the card through the holes in the tree.

3. Thread the needle with the green yarn. Pull the yarn so that the ends of it are even. Do not tie a knot.

4. To stitch the tree, start from the front of the card at the top of the tree. Push the needle DOWN through hole 1 and pull the needle and yarn through the hole, leaving a "tail" of yarn on the front of the card. Pull the needle UP through hole 2. Cut the yarn, leaving a "tail" of yarn at that hole, too. Make stitches in the same way across the middle and bottom rows of the tree.

5. Draw and color a trunk and ornaments on the tree and gaily wrapped presents under the tree. Stick a shiny star on top of the tree. Sign your card and send it to someone you love.

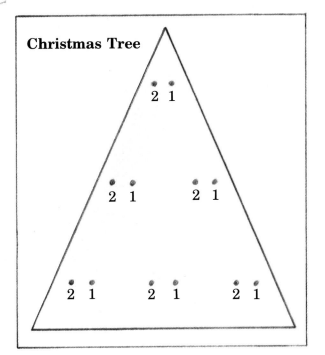

Christmas Tree

Quickie Quackers

It takes just minutes to make duck puppets for presents. Make a hand puppet or a handful of finger puppets. You'll need felt, feathers, wiggly-eyes, and glue. You haven't any feathers? Check the zoo!

You will need:
pencil
tracing paper
scissors
white or brown felt
gold felt
white glue
feathers
plastic wiggly-eyes
felt-tip marker (or paint pen)

1. Trace the body, wing, bill, and foot patterns for the duck puppet that you want to make. Cut out the patterns. Draw around the body and the wing two times each on white or brown felt. Draw around the bill one time and the foot two times on gold felt. Cut out the felt pieces.

2. Glue the feet and the feather onto the top of one felt body piece. On the other body piece, put glue along the side and top edges, but not the bottom edge. Press the body piece with the glue onto the body piece with the feet and feather.

3. Glue on the wiggly-eyes. Draw dots on the bill with the felt-tip marker. Glue the bill and the wings in place. Let the glue dry—and you'll have a puppet that is ready for action!

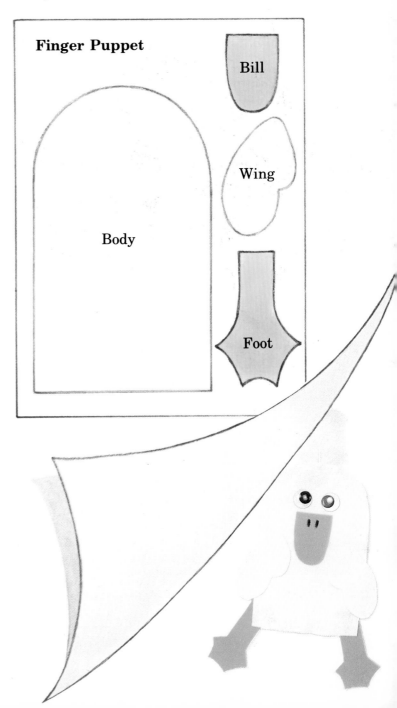

Finger Puppet

Bill

Wing

Body

Foot

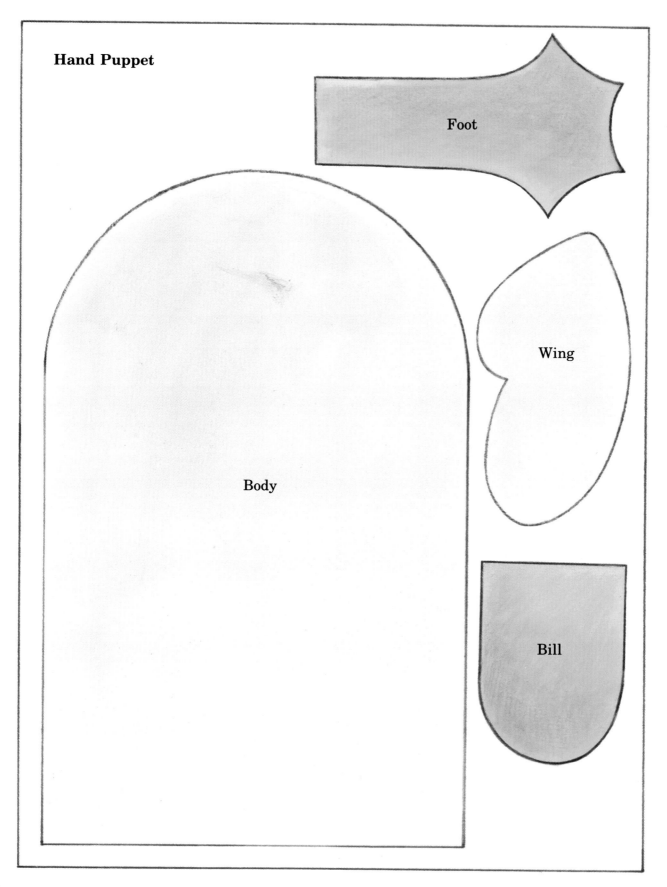

Hand Puppet

Foot

Wing

Body

Bill

42

Cookie Creations

Make these cookie pins and necklaces for your best girl friends. You will not need to bake, because the cookies come ready-to-wear—straight from the grocery store!

For safety's sake: Give these pins and necklaces only to friends who are old enough to know that when cookies have glue and pin backs on them, they are not to be eaten.

Ginger Man Necklaces

You will need:
white glue
red candy hearts
Pepperidge Farm Ginger Man cookies
 (mmm . . . better buy two bags!)
narrow satin ribbon (about 24″ for each
 necklace)

1. Glue the red hearts on the Ginger Man cookies. Glue the ends of a satin ribbon to the back of each cookie. Let the glue dry.

Animal Cracker Pin Pals

You will need:
white glue
tiny red and green satin bows
animal crackers (better buy two bags of
 these cookies, too!)
pin backs

1. Glue the bows onto the front of the animal crackers. Let the glue dry. Glue the pin backs onto the back of the animal crackers and let the glue dry.

Tub-Time Toys

If you have a baby brother who doesn't like taking a bath, maybe he needs some company! Give him a bunch of these tub-time toys—ducks, alligators, and all sorts of fish that you cut from colorful sponges.

You will need:
pencil
tracing paper
scissors
felt-tip marker with permanent ink
soft sponges

1. Trace the patterns for the duck, alligator, and fish on tracing paper. Cut out the patterns.

2. Use the felt-tip marker to draw around each pattern on a dry sponge.

3. Soak the sponges in water and then squeeze them as dry as you can. Cut out the toys with your scissors, cutting inside the marker line and squeezing the sponge as you cut.

Sailboat Desk Set

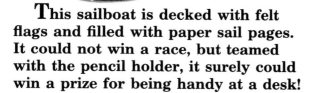

This sailboat is decked with felt flags and filled with paper sail pages. It could not win a race, but teamed with the pencil holder, it surely could win a prize for being handy at a desk!

You will need:
1 (6-ounce) frozen juice can
Tacky Glue
clothesline cord
pencil
tracing paper
scissors
red felt
blue felt
white poster paper
hole punch
typing paper

Pencil Holder

1. Cover the outside of the orange juice can with glue.

2. Starting at the bottom of the can, tightly wrap the cord around the can about four times. Push the rows of cord together. Wrap the cord around the can four more times and push the rows together. Keep wrapping the cord and pushing the rows together (and adding more glue if you need it) until you have covered the can with cord. Cut the cord and glue the end to the can.

3. Cut a piece of cord that is long enough to wrap around the can one time. Glue the cord on top of the last row of wrapped cord so that the ends meet on the back of the can. Let the glue dry.

4. Trace the pattern for the anchor on tracing paper. Cut out the anchor and draw around it on felt. Cut out the felt anchor. Glue the anchor and other decorations onto the pencil holder.

Sailboat Pad

1. Trace the outline of the sailboat on tracing paper. Cut out the boat and draw around it two times on white poster paper. Cut out the two boats. Use these for the front and back of the pad.

2. Trace the patterns for the flag, mast, and boat bottoms. Cut out the patterns and draw around them on felt. Cut out the felt pieces. Glue them onto one of the poster paper boats, looking at the drawing to see where the flag and mast go. Make poster paper circles for portholes with a hole punch. Glue the circles onto the boat.

3. To make sail-shaped pages for the pad, trace the pattern and cut it out. Draw around the pattern on a sheet of typing paper. Place a small stack of typing paper under the sheet with the sail on it. Cut around the sail. Cut small stacks of sail-shaped pages in this way, until you have enough to fill the pad.

4. On the decorated boat, punch a hole under the flag, looking at the pattern to see exactly where the hole should be. Punch a hole in the plain boat, in the same place. Then punch holes in the sail-shaped pages.

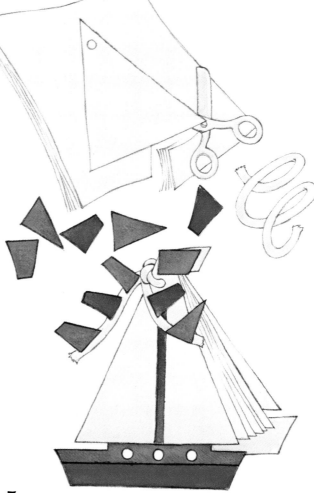

5. Sandwich the paper sails between the two boats. Cut a piece of clothesline cord and string it through the holes. Tie a knot. Cut flags from the felt and glue them onto the cord.

48

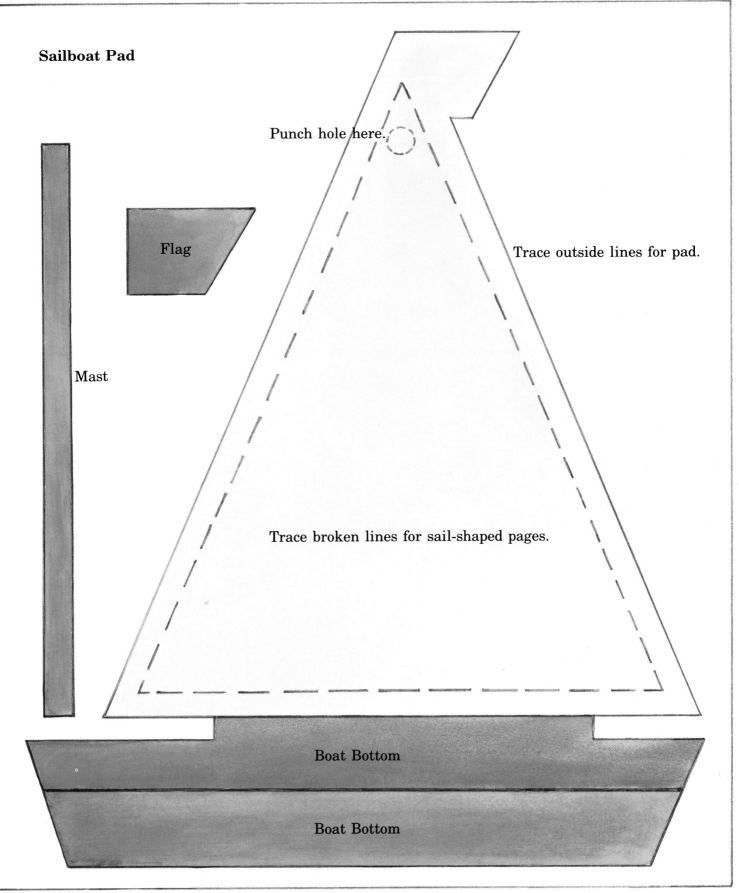

Sailboat Pad

Flag

Mast

Punch hole here.

Trace outside lines for pad.

Trace broken lines for sail-shaped pages.

Boat Bottom

Boat Bottom

Color an Ice Candle

One of these lacy-looking candles would be a nice present for your teacher. Make the candle short or tall, round or square—in the color that she likes best!

For safety's sake: A hot stove and hot wax can be very dangerous, so ask your mom to melt and pour the wax for these candles. Use an electric stove—not a gas stove—and do not allow the wax to boil. Be sure to follow the instructions step-by-step—CAREFULLY!

Before you start: Follow the instructions below to make a tall candle like the purple one in the picture. To make a round candle like the yellow one, follow the same instructions, but use a 12-ounce juice can and two bars of paraffin wax. To make a short candle like the green one, use a pint-sized milk carton and two bars of paraffin wax.

You will need:
empty (quart-sized) milk carton
candle wicking
pencil
scissors
cracked ice
3 bars of paraffin wax
empty coffee can
cooking pan
crayon
old wooden spoon

1. Open the top of the milk carton all the way. Tie one end of the candle wicking around the middle of the pencil. Hold the pencil even with the top of the carton. From the candle wicking, cut a wick that is as long as the carton. Rest the pencil across the top of the carton, with the wick hanging down the middle.

2. Fill the carton with cracked ice and place it in the freezer.

3. Put the three bars of paraffin wax in an empty coffee can. Place the can in a cooking pan that is half-filled with water. Put the pan on the stove. Ask your mom to turn on the stove, setting the heat on "very low." Heat the pan until all of the wax has melted. Remind your mom to turn off the stove.

4. Remove the wrapper from a crayon. Break the crayon into small pieces and drop them one at a time into the melted wax. Stir the mixture with an old wooden spoon. Add pieces of crayon until the wax turns the color that you would like for the candle.

5. Take the milk carton out of the freezer. Ask your mom to pour the melted wax over the ice in the milk carton, filling it almost to the top. As the ice melts, pour off the water. Set the carton aside until the wax hardens.

6. Place the carton in the sink and tear the sides of the carton from the candle. Untie the wick and trim it with scissors.

On Your Mark!

Use scraps of felt and brightly colored ribbon to make these bookmarks. Give them to classmates who like to read.

You will need:
pencil
tracing paper
scissors
felt
ribbon
white glue
paint pen

1. Trace the patterns for the bookmarks. Cut out the patterns. Draw around each pattern two times on felt. Cut out the felt pieces.

2. Glue the trim on the kite, football, flower, heart, and tennis racket. Let the glue dry.

3. For each bookmark, glue the matching felt pieces to the ends of a ribbon, making the back of the bookmark look just like the front. Let the glue dry.

4. Use a paint pen to make markings on the balls and the tennis racket. Tie short ribbons to one long ribbon to make the kite tail.

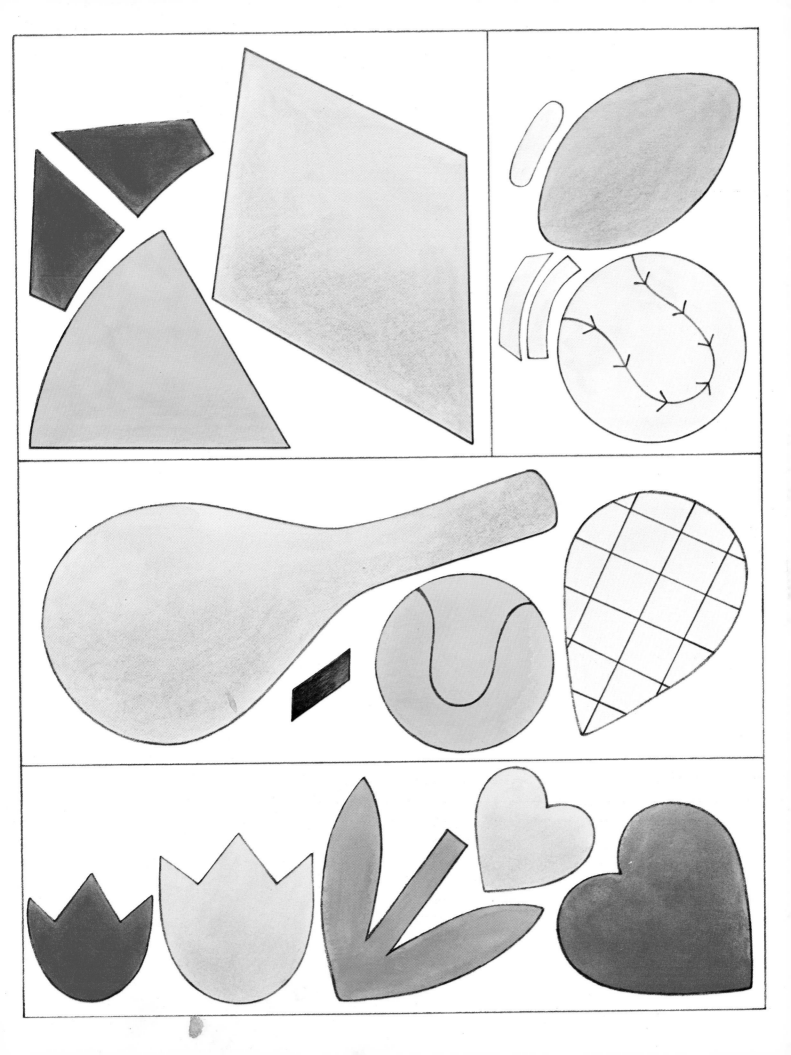

Super Surprise Balls

These presents are fun to wrap and fun to open. Won't your friends be surprised when they find what's inside!

Before you start: Decide whether to make the Angel, Santa, or Snowman. Follow the five steps under Wrapping and Painting the Ball. Then follow the steps under the name of the surprise ball that you have decided to make.

You will need:

packages of crepe paper in different colors, including pale pink, red, white, and black
ruler
pencil
scissors
5 very small surprises
paper towels
white glue
acrylic paint (white, red, blue, and black)
small paintbrush
water for rinsing the paintbrush
waxed paper

For the Angel: tracing paper, white poster paper, gold paint, yarn, 12″ x 6″ piece of cardboard, ribbon, gold-fringed chenille stem, pink pom-pom

For the Santa: red pom-pom, white yarn, 6″ x 6″ piece of cardboard, white pom-pom

For the Snowman: pom-pom, ribbon

Level 2

Wrapping and Painting the Ball

1. Cut six 1″ strips (crosswise) from the different colors of folded crepe paper. Unfold the strips.

2. Wrap the first surprise in one strip of crepe paper. Hold the second surprise next to the first one and wrap them both in another strip of crepe paper. Add the other three surprises the same way, one at a time, to make a lumpy ball.

3. Make the ball smoother by wrapping it in a paper towel. Wrap the ball with the last strip of crepe paper and then another paper towel.

4. If you're making the Angel or Santa, cut three 1″ strips (crosswise) from pale pink crepe paper. If you're making the Snowman, cut three 1″ strips from white crepe paper. Unfold the strips and wrap them tightly and neatly, one at a time, around the ball of wrapped surprises. Glue the end of the last strip to the back of the ball. Let the glue dry.

5. Lightly draw two circles for eyes and two circles for cheeks on the front of the ball. Paint the eyes white. Mix red paint with a little white paint on waxed paper, to make pink paint. Paint the cheeks pink. Let the paint dry. Then, to add a glow, paint a tiny white dot on each cheek.

Paint two blue circles inside the white circles. When the blue circles are dry, paint little black circles in the middle of them. Paint black eyelashes and eyebrows. Then paint a tiny white dot on each blue circle for a twinkle. If you're making the Angel or Snowman, paint a happy red smile from one cheek to the other. Let the paint dry.

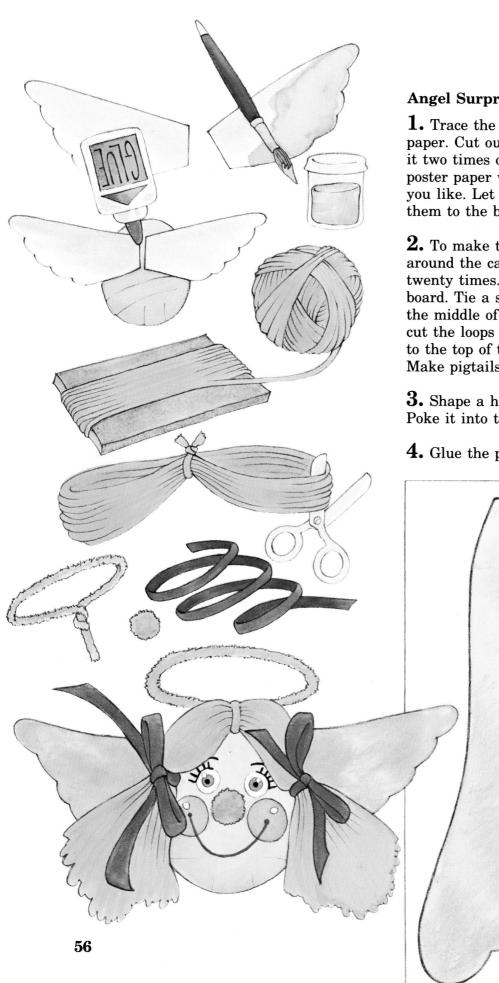

Angel Surprise Ball

1. Trace the Angel's wing on tracing paper. Cut out the wing and draw around it two times on poster paper. Cut out the poster paper wings. Paint them gold, if you like. Let the wings dry and then glue them to the back of the ball.

2. To make the hair, loop the yarn around the cardboard (lengthwise) about twenty times. Slip the yarn off the cardboard. Tie a short piece of yarn around the middle of the looped yarn and then cut the loops at either end. Glue the yarn to the top of the ball. Let the glue dry. Make pigtails and tie them with ribbons.

3. Shape a halo with the chenille stem. Poke it into the back of the ball.

4. Glue the pom-pom—you "nose" where!

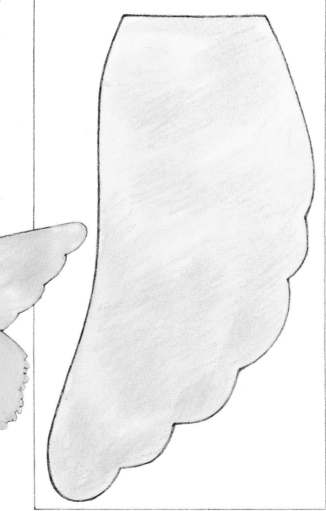

56

Santa Surprise Ball

1. Glue on the red pom-pom for a nose "like a cherry."

2. To make Santa's beard, loop the yarn around the cardboard about twenty times. Slip the yarn off the cardboard. Tie a short piece of yarn around the middle of the looped yarn and then cut the loops on either end. Glue the yarn beard under the pom-pom nose. Glue some of the yarn across Santa's cheeks so that the beard will look full. Let the glue dry.

3. For Santa's hat, cut a 12″ x 7″ piece of red crepe paper and a 12″ x 4″ piece of white crepe paper. Wrap the piece of red crepe paper around the ball. Fold under the ends of the paper and glue them to the back of the ball. Fold the piece of white crepe paper to make a hatband. Wrap it around the bottom of the hat and glue the ends to the back of the ball. Glue the white pom-pom onto the tip of the hat. Pull down the top of the hat and glue it to one side of the ball. Let the glue dry.

Snowman Surprise Ball

1. Glue on the pom-pom nose.

2. To make the Snowman's hat, cut a piece that is 10″ x 7″ from black crepe paper. Fold up the bottom for the brim. Wrap the piece of crepe paper around the ball. Fold under the ends to make the hat fit and then glue the ends to the back of the ball. If the hat is too tall, cut off the top.

3. Tie the ribbon around the hat and make a bow on the side.

PARENTS' WORKSHOP
Great Gifts for Children

Tacky Tops

Dot a sweatshirt and accessories with tack tops and what do you have? Instant interest, color, and kid-appeal!

You will need:
small screwdriver
plastic-coated thumbtacks
waxed paper
sweatshirt (prewash to remove sizing)
Quik Glue
pair of tennis socks
visor

1. Using the screwdriver, remove the tops from the tacks by gently prying the lip of the tops from the underside of the tacks.

2. Slide waxed paper inside the sweatshirt. Arrange the tack tops on the sweatshirt in a pleasing pattern and then glue them in place. Press firmly on the tops several times to ensure adhesion. Gently remove the waxed paper. Hang the sweatshirt and allow glue to dry overnight.

3. Glue tack tops on the socks and visor. Let dry overnight.

Note: Wait at least three days after gluing the tack tops to a garment before washing it. Machine-wash in cold water on the permanent-press cycle. Hang to dry—do not machine-dry!

Kooky Caps

Topped with a snake or decked with hearts, these out-of-the-ordinary caps are guaranteed to be popular with kids. If you have a scrap bag, be sure to check it before heading to the store with the "you will need" list. An orange snake will look just as sneaky as the green one, and hot-colored, polka-dotted hearts will look just as sweet as the solid, pastel ones. In other words . . . on a kooky cap, anything goes!

Jungle Cap

You will need:
Craft Bondex in kelly green, brown, and
  forest green
blue baseball cap
10″ x 15″ piece of kelly green fabric
polyester stuffing
2 black beads
scrap of red felt

1. Trace and cut out the patterns for the
grass, palm tree top, and palm tree trunk.
Cut three panels of grass from kelly
green Craft Bondex. Cut two palm tree
trunks from brown Craft Bondex; reverse
the trunk and cut three more. Cut two
palm tree tops from forest green Craft
Bondex; reverse the top and cut two more.
Following the package instructions, apply
the grass and then the trunks around the
bottom of the cap. Cut one palm tree top
in half to make two small tops; apply the
five tops to the trunks.

2. Trace and cut out the pattern for the
snake, adding ¼″ seam allowance. Cut
two snakes from the kelly green fabric.
With right sides together, pin the snakes
and sew, leaving opening as marked.
Turn and stuff the snake; sew the opening closed.

  Cut "spots" from the remaining brown
Craft Bondex and apply them to the
snake's back. Sew on beads for eyes. Cut
a red felt tongue and sew it to the snake.
Tack the underside of the snake to the
top of the cap.

Sweetheart Cap

You will need:
lavender baseball cap
small pieces of yellow, pink, and blue
  fabric
polyester stuffing
2 yards each (⅛″-wide) yellow, pink, blue,
  and lavender ribbon
12 heart buttons

1. Trace and cut out the heart pattern.
Cut four hearts each from the yellow and
blue fabric and two hearts from the pink
fabric. With right sides together, pin the
matching hearts. Sew, using ¼″ seam allowances and leaving openings as
marked. Turn and stuff the hearts; sew
the openings closed.

2. For each stuffed heart, cut an 8″
length of ribbon in a contrasting color.
Tie the ribbons into bows. Place a heart
button over the center of each bow and
sew both the button and the bow to the
top of a stuffed heart. Tack the five
stuffed hearts to the front of the cap,
above the visor.

3. Cut a 15″ length of each color of ribbon. Arrange the ribbons into bows (Figure A) and top the bows with a single
button. Sew the button and bows to the
top center of the cap.

4. For the bows that go around the
crown of the cap, cut three 8″ ribbons
from each color. Sort the ribbons into six
pairs, mixing the colors in each pair. Arrange the pairs of ribbons into bows, top
the bows with a button, and sew the but-
ton-topped bows around the crown of the
cap, spacing them evenly.

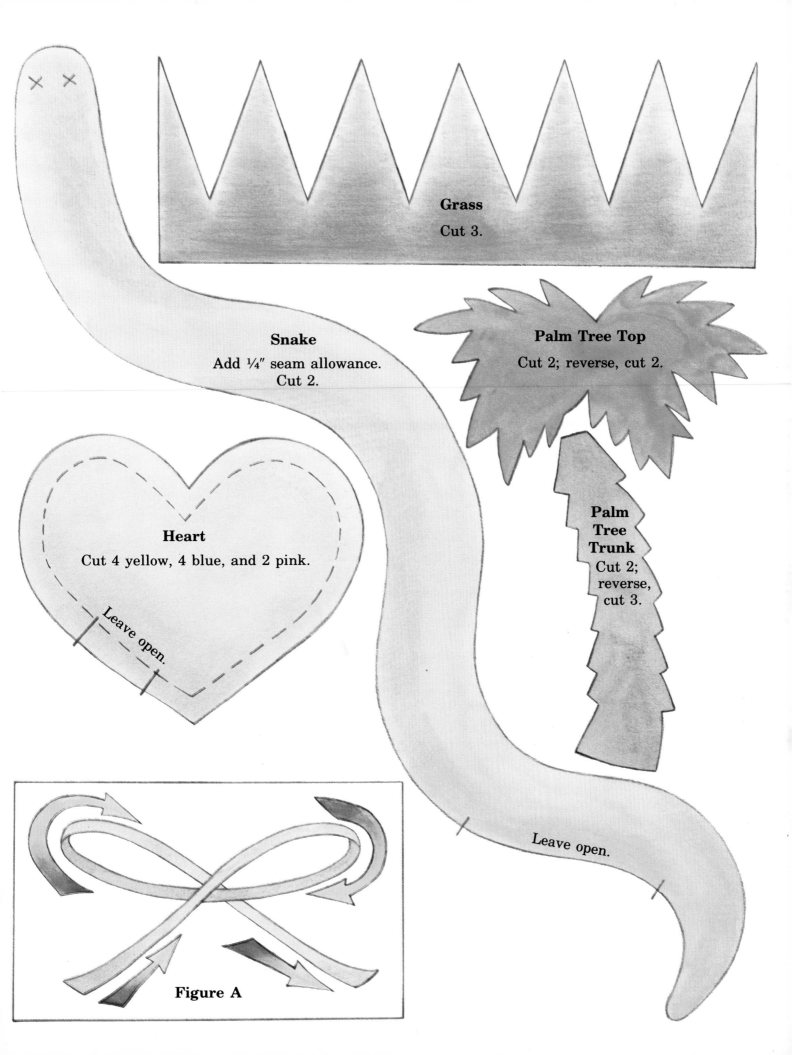

Grass

Cut 3.

Snake

Add ¼″ seam allowance.
Cut 2.

Palm Tree Top

Cut 2; reverse, cut 2.

Palm Tree Trunk

Cut 2; reverse, cut 3.

Heart

Cut 4 yellow, 4 blue, and 2 pink.

Leave open.

Leave open.

Figure A

Cross-Stitched Choo-Choo

Paired with a crisp white shirt, these cross-stitched overalls make a cute suit for a tot to wear on a special occasion—a birthday party, picture-taking day at school, or when the circus comes to town. The chart for stitching the design is simple to follow, and the design itself is fun to work. And because the overalls are purchased, you can finish this project quickly—and get busy on another!

64

You will need:
pair of red overalls
14-count waste canvas (about 3″ x 7″)
embroidery floss (in colors indicated by
 color key)

1. Mark the center of both the bib of the overalls and the waste canvas. Place the waste canvas over the bib, aligning the centers. Baste the edges of the canvas to the bib and then baste from top to bottom and from side to side, through the center of the canvas.

2. Using two strands of floss in the colors suggested in color key, work the design in cross-stitch, beginning at the center.

When you have finished, outline the bars on the cage, using backstitch and one strand of green. Outline the following as marked on the graph, using backstitch and one strand of brown-black: on engine, outline cowcatcher, bell, yellow stripes,

window and panes, canopy; on middle car, outline giraffe, top and bottom of cage; on caboose, outline rail, window and panes, canopy.

For the giraffe's horn, make a back-stitch and a French knot, using two strands of brown-black. Use two strands of green to embroider an X in the center of each wheel on the middle car.

3. Clip and remove the basting threads. Saturate the canvas with water and then use tweezers to pull the canvas, thread by thread, from under the stitches.

Color Key (DMC)

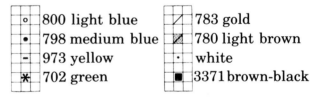

○ 800 light blue	╱ 783 gold
• 798 medium blue	▨ 780 light brown
- 973 yellow	· white
✳ 702 green	■ 3371 brown-black

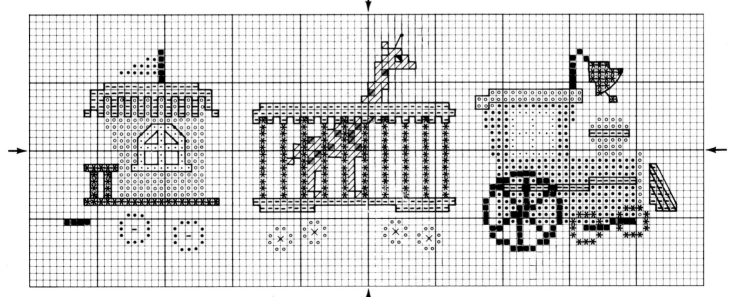

Froggy Backpack

Designed with beginners in mind, this roomy backpack will hold all of the necessities for school: a book or two, paper and pencil, a snack or lunch, and—of course—something for show-and-tell.

You will need:
3/4 yard (45″-wide) heavy-weight orange fabric
2 yards of natural woven belting
2 yards (⅝″-wide) orange grosgrain ribbon
2 pairs (1″) D-rings
8″ square of green polka-dot fabric
⅓ yard (36″-wide) solid green fabric
6″ x 8″ piece of yellow fabric
Craft Bondex in red and yellow
polyester stuffing
5″ piece of black string
white glue
2 (½″) black buttons
2 pairs of Velcro fasteners (medium duty)

1. From the orange fabric, cut a rectangle that is 17″ x 38″, cutting so that one 17″ side is on the selvage. From remaining orange fabric, cut two 4″ x 11½″ strips (for sides of pack), cutting so that one of the 4″ ends of each strip is on the selvage.

2. On 17″ x 38″ piece of fabric, turn under selvage edge ½″ and sew. Turn under opposite edge ¼″; press and sew. Turn under same edge ½″ and sew.

On the wrong side of the fabric, mark 11″ from the double-folded edge, on the left-hand and right-hand sides. Mark 3″ above the 11″ marks. With right sides together, center and pin the raw-edged ends of the side strips to the pack, between the marks. Sew, between the marks only, using a ½″ seam allowance. (Figure A.)

With right sides together, pin the 11″ sides of the side strips to front and back of pack; sew, using ½″ seam allowance. Trim seams and clip corners. Zigzag the raw edges of the seams together.

On the front flap, zigzag along the raw edges and then turn them under ½″; press and sew. Turn the pack right side out.

3. Cut two 34″ lengths of belting and two 34″ lengths of ribbon. Pin the ribbons down the center of the belting strips and sew, stitching along the edges of the ribbon. Fold under one end of each belting strip ¼″ and sew. Slip a pair of D-rings on each of the other ends. Fold under the ends 1″ and sew (with rings inside fold).

Fold the belting strips in half and mark the middle. Mark 3″ above and 3″ below the middle mark. Center strips 6″ apart, ribbon-side down, on back of pack. Sew strips to pack across the marks, sewing back and forth several times.

4. Trace and cut out the patterns for the frog, adding ¼″ seam allowances to the head, front and back legs, and tie. Cut

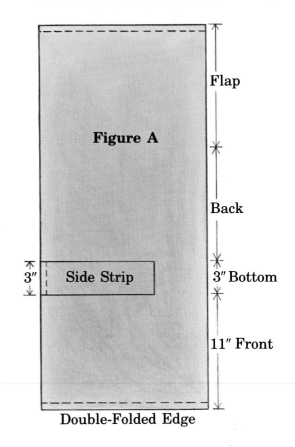

Figure A

Flap

Back

Side Strip

3″

3″ Bottom

11″ Front

Double-Folded Edge

one body from the green polka-dot fabric. Cut two heads, four front legs, and four back legs from the solid green fabric. Cut two ties from the yellow fabric. Cut the eyelids and cheeks from Craft Bondex.

5. Fold under bottom edge of the body ½″ and press. Pin bottom of body to center front edge of flap. Using satin-stitch, sew top and sides of body to the flap, leaving the bottom open. Remove the pins. Stuff body lightly and whipstitch bottom to edge of the flap.

6. With right sides together, pin pieces for legs. Sew, leaving openings as marked. Turn and stuff; sew openings closed. Sew front legs to top and back legs to bottom of body. Tack the knees.

7. Sew pieces for tie, leaving opening as marked. Turn tie and sew opening closed. Satin-stitch the knot as marked. Tack top of tie to tops of front legs.

8. With right sides together, pin the pieces for the head. Sew, leaving opening as marked. Turn head right side out and press. Stuff; sew opening closed.

Following instructions on Craft Bondex package, apply cheeks and eyelids to head. Glue on string for the mouth and sew on buttons for eyes. Tack head to tops of front legs and to center of flap.

9. Sew one pair of Velcro fasteners to underside of flap and one pair to front of pack.

Body

Cut 1.

Leave bottom open for stuffing.

Leave open.

Front Leg

Add ¼"
seam
allowance.
Cut 4.

Leave open.

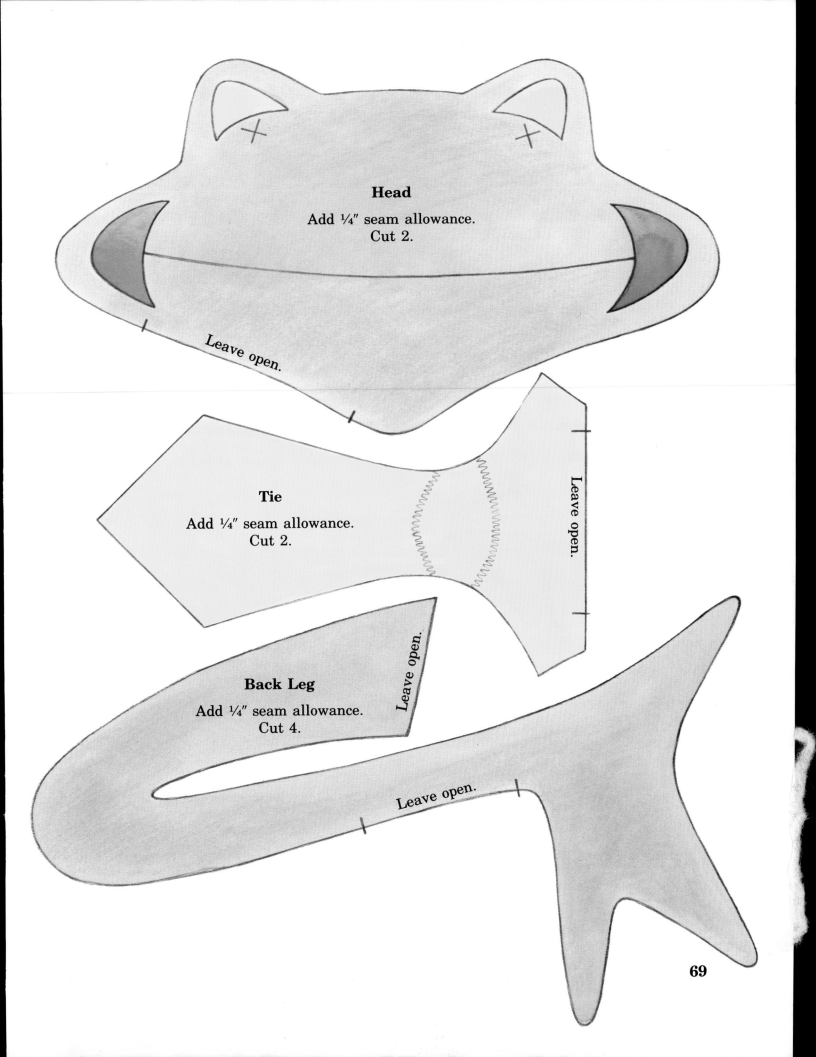

Head

Add ¼″ seam allowance.
Cut 2.

Leave open.

Tie

Add ¼″ seam allowance.
Cut 2.

Leave open.

Back Leg

Add ¼″ seam allowance.
Cut 4.

Leave open.

Leave open.

69

Sailboat Sweater

Three cheers for the red, white, and blue—and for duplicate-stitch embroidery, which is the way the sailboats were "knitted" onto these smart little sweaters.

To apply the embroidery, use yarn that is of a similar weight to that which was used to knit the sweater. (Cotton floss can be used to stitch the design onto a cotton sweater.) Pull your stitches carefully so that the embroidery completely covers the knitted stitches without altering the tension.

You will need:
sweater (ready-made or hand-knitted)
tapestry needle
yarn in red, white, blue, and yellow

1. Match center of sweater to center of design as marked on graph.

Figure A

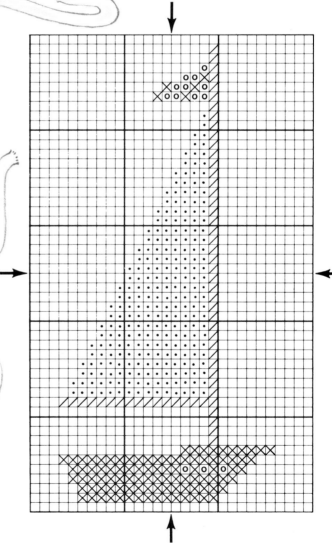

2. Thread the needle with yarn. Starting from the wrong side of the sweater and leaving about a 4″ tail, pull the needle up through the stitch that is below the one to be covered. (Figure A.) Pass the needle from right to left under the stitch that is above the one to be covered. (Figure A.) Then reinsert the needle into the stitch through which you originally pulled the needle. (Figure B.)

3. Follow the graph to complete the design. As you finish with each color, weave the ends of the yarn through several stitches on the back of the sweater.

Figure B

Color Key

✕	red
╱	yellow
○	blue
·	white

71

For a Budding Artist

Delight a young artist with an easel, an apron, and a boxful of supplies. If you've done some woodworking and you have a few basic tools, constructing the easel will be simple. Make the wipe-clean, vinyl apron—in minutes—to keep spatters and spills off clothing. And for hours of creative fun, fill a plastic caddy with all that is needed for drawing, doodling, and dabbling in the arts.

Making the Easel

You will need:

tracing paper
35″ x 28″ (½″) best-grade plywood
yardstick
electric saber saw
2 (8′) 1 x 2s
18″ x 24″ pad of newsprint
¼″ electric drill with ³⁄₁₆″ bit
2 (2½″-long and ³⁄₁₆″-diameter) slot-head bolts with wing nuts
screwdriver
3 (3″-long and ³⁄₁₆″-diameter) slot-head bolts with washers and nuts
sandpaper
wood filler
paintbrush
enamel undercoat
carbon paper
high-gloss enamel paint (assorted colors)
artist's brushes (assorted sizes)
36″ common chain (with links large enough to fit around ³⁄₁₆″ bolt)

1. Trace the pattern for the bear, including the features. Cut out the pattern.

2. Turn the plywood with the rough side up and draw a line from side to side, 6¾″ from and parallel to one of the 28″ sides. Reverse the pattern and place it on the plywood, about 3″ from the right-hand side, with the straight edge on the line. Starting at the line, draw only around the part of the bear that extends above the line. (Do not draw around the part below the line.) Using the saber saw, cut along the straight line up to the outline of the bear, around the outline of the bear, and along the remaining straight line.

3. Cut an 18″ block from one of the 1 x 2s. In the 2″ side of the block, center and drill a ³⁄₁₆″ hole 4″ from each end.

4. Place the plywood with smooth side up on a flat work surface. Center the pad of newsprint on the plywood and place the 18″ block on top of the pad, aligning top edges. With assistance in holding block and pad in place, pass the drill through each hole in the block and drill holes through the pad and plywood.

5. For the stand, cut two 48″ lengths (front legs), one 47″ length (back leg), and one 27½″ length (crosspiece) from the 1 x 2s.

6. In the 2″ side of the crosspiece, center and drill a ³⁄₁₆″ hole 5″ from each end. In the 1″ side of each front leg, center and drill a ³⁄₁₆″ hole 21½″ from the bottom of the leg, being careful to hold the drill at a 90° angle to the wood. Place the cross-piece over the front legs and align the holes. Insert a 3″ bolt in each set of holes but do not secure bolts with nuts.

7. Lay the crosspiece (with front legs attached) face down on the work surface. Place the back leg between the front legs so that it is over the exact center of the crosspiece. With the tops of the front legs resting on the work surface, raise the top of the back leg ⅜″ from the work surface. With assistance in holding the legs, drill a ³⁄₁₆″ hole through all three legs, 1″ from

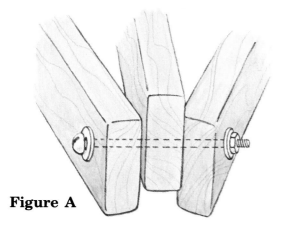

Figure A

the top. (See Figure A, above, for position of legs and hole.) Insert a 3″ bolt and secure with a washer and nut.

8. Sand all cut edges and rough surfaces. Use wood filler where needed; allow to dry and sand again. Apply enamel undercoat to the wood pieces and let dry.

Trace the paintbrush and paint circle. Use carbon paper to transfer tracings of paintbrush, paint circle, and bear's features onto easel. Using photograph as a color guide, paint the easel. Let dry.

9. Attach block and pad to easel with the 2½″ bolts and secure with wing nuts. Put last links of the 36″ chain onto the bolts holding the crosspiece to the front legs and secure each with a washer and nut.

**Making the
Art Apron
and Box**

You will need:
tape measure
super-bonding glue

Note: An 18″ x 22½″ apron will fit most children ages five to six. To make an apron for a younger or older child, adjust the dimensions of the vinyl accordingly.

For the Apron: brown paper for pattern, 18″ x 22½″ of vinyl, 1 package bias tape (about 3 yards), scraps of vinyl for hearts

For the Box: plastic caddy (from hardware or variety store), 2 yards (1″-wide) grosgrain ribbon, scraps of vinyl in same colors as modeling clay, plastic containers with tops, modeling clay, cellulose sponges (for sponge painting), assorted art supplies

1. Draw the pattern for the apron on brown paper. Cut out the pattern and use it to cut a vinyl apron.

Cut a 6¼″ strip of bias tape and sew it across the top of the apron. For ties, cut two 48″ strips of bias tape. Sew the strips along the curves, allowing about 18″ of tape at the waist and 18″ at the neck, on each side of the apron. Knot ends of ties.

Trace the heart pattern. Cut five hearts from vinyl. Glue or machine-stitch the hearts along the bottom of the apron.

2. Cut and then glue a piece of grosgrain ribbon around sides of the plastic caddy. Cut a 24″ piece of ribbon and tie it into a bow. Glue bow to ribbon on caddy.

Cut circles from scraps of vinyl and glue them to the plastic container tops. Fill each container with modeling clay that is the same color as the circle on the top. Cut the sponges into circles, squares, and other shapes. Place these and other art supplies in the caddy.

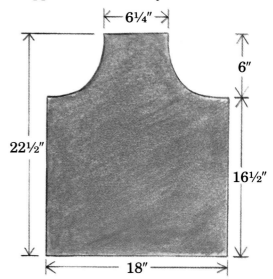

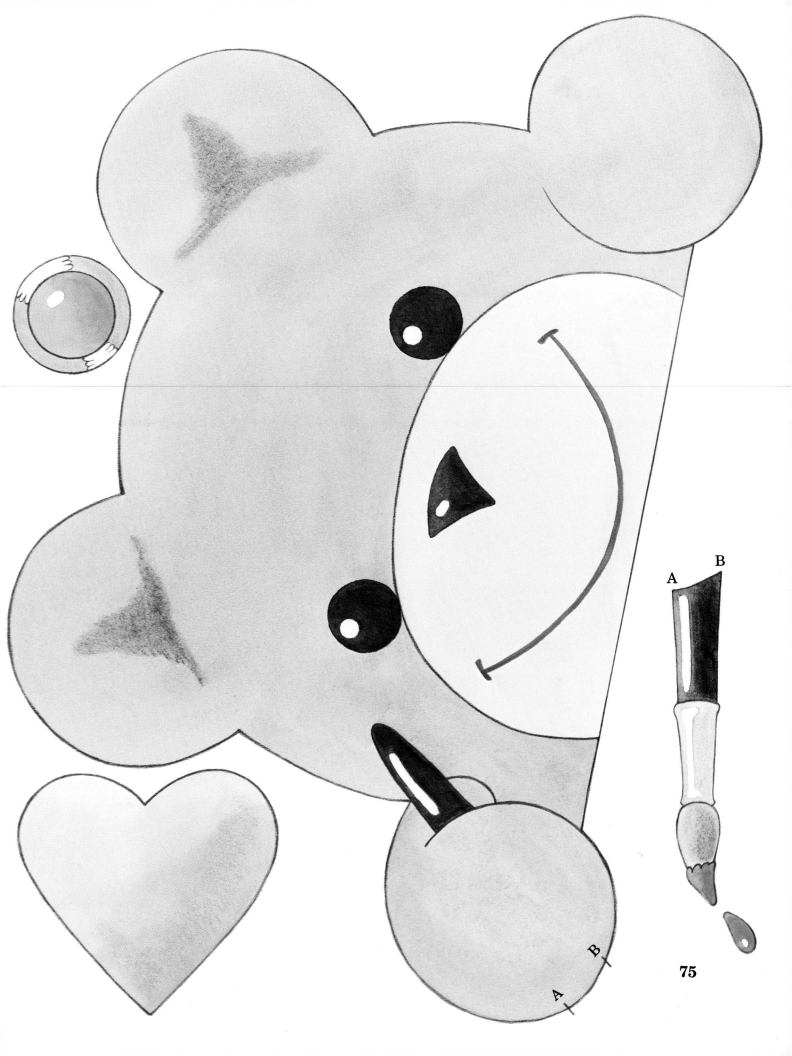

A

B

A

B

75

Dolly's Closet

What little girl wouldn't jump for joy to find this doll-sized closet under the tree on Christmas morning? The instructions that follow are for making the closet, hangers, and hat and shoe boxes. Perhaps Santa will bring a pretty new doll—and a closetful of new doll dresses.

Making the Closet

You will need:

tracing paper
1½' x 3' (¾") best-grade plywood
yardstick
wood glue
electric saber saw
sandpaper
¼" electric drill with ½" paddle bit and
   ⁹⁄₆₄" drill bit
C-clamp
6 (1½" to 2") #8 wood screws
screwdriver
18" (½") wooden dowel
coping saw (optional)
¼" plywood (for hangers)
wood filler
paintbrush
enamel undercoat
high-gloss enamel paint (white and
   assorted colors)
carbon paper
artist's brushes (assorted sizes)

1. Trace the pattern for the doll (including features) onto tracing paper. Cut out the pattern. Mark the front A and the back B.

2. On the back (rough side) of the ¾" plywood, draw around side A of the doll, then side B, for the closet ends. Measure and mark a 7¾" x 18" rectangle for the closet floor and two 1" squares for blocks to hold the wooden dowel. Using the saber saw, carefully cut out the pieces of wood. Sand the edges.

3. Drill a ½" hole through the exact center of each square block. Glue a block to the back (rough side) of each doll, near the top of the head. Use a C-clamp to hold the pieces together until the glue is dry.

4. On the front (smooth side) of each doll, draw a line from side to side ¼" from the bottom. Drill three countersink holes in each doll, spacing the holes evenly along the line.

With assistance, position one of the dolls (smooth side out) at one end of the closet floor, aligning the bottom edges. Pass the drill through each countersink hole and drill a ⁹⁄₆₄" hole in the floor. Repeat with second doll at other end of floor.

With doll in place, insert wood screws in one end and tighten. Put glue on one end of the dowel and insert it in the hole in the wood block on back of the doll. Glue the other end of the dowel to the second doll and then secure doll to floor with screws.

5. Transfer the pattern for the dress hangers to the ¼" plywood. Using the saber saw or a coping saw, cut out the hangers.

6. Use wood filler to fill any cracks or holes in the wood pieces and let dry. Sand all of the rough surfaces. Apply the enamel undercoat. Let dry and lightly sand again. Paint the entire closet white. When dry, use carbon paper to transfer the features onto the dolls. Paint the dolls, using the photograph as a color guide.

Making the Hat and Shoe Boxes

You will need:
poster paper
yardstick
print wrapping paper (heavy)
cellophane tape
tissue paper
oatmeal box
white glue
compass
masking tape
about ⅔ yard ribbon
½ yard cording

1. To make a shoe box, transfer the patterns for the top and bottom of the box onto cardboard and cut them out. Fold the cardboard pieces as marked and tape the corners. From the print paper, cut a 3¾" x 5¼" piece for wrapping the top and a 5½" x 7" piece for wrapping the bottom. Wrap the box, taping the edges of the paper to the inside. Crumple a small piece of tissue paper and place it inside the box.

2. For bottom of hatbox, cut the oatmeal box to a height of 5". Cut a 7" x 18" piece of print paper. Mix two tablespoons of glue with one tablespoon of water. Cover the box with a thin layer of the glue mixture and apply the paper, leaving 1" of excess paper at the top and 1" at the bottom. Turn under the side edge of the paper and glue it to the box. Fold down and glue the top edge to the inside of the box. Glue the bottom edge to the underside of the box.

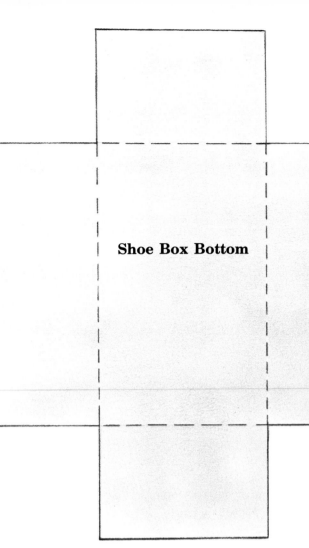

Shoe Box Bottom

Shoe Box Top

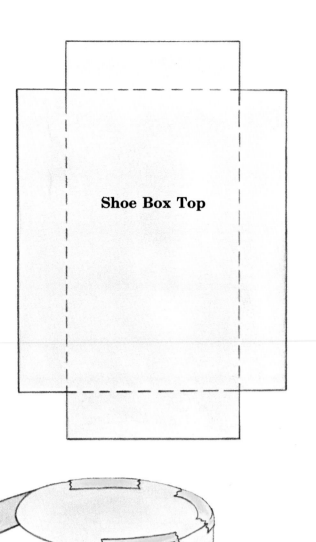

3. For the hatbox top, cut a 5½″ circle and a 17½″ x 1½″ strip from cardboard. Attach the strip to the circle with masking tape. (Figure A.) Cut a 5½″ circle and an 18″ x 2″ strip from print paper. Glue the paper strip to the cardboard strip, overlapping and turning under the excess paper. Glue the paper circle onto the cardboard circle. To hide the raw edges, glue a piece of ribbon around the top. Add a bow. Let glue dry.

Figure A

4. To finish the hatbox, paint the inside with acrylic paint and let dry. Measure 1¾″ down from the top edge. Punch a hole in one side, then the other side. Push the ends of the cord through the holes (from the outside of the box) and tie a knot in each end. Crumple tissue paper and place it inside the box.

To make pattern for ends of closet,
align Xs on this page with Xs on
opposite page and trace doll.

Friendship Pillowcases

Signing autograph books and hounds may be out, but signing pillowcases is in! And these were painted with that purpose in mind. Collecting signatures on them is a great, up-to-date way for kids to remember who shared the secrets at the last pajama party or who bunked in their cabin while they were at camp.

You will need:
pillowcase
felt-tip marker
tracing paper
water-soluble pen
acrylic paint (Mars Black, Titanium White, Prism Violet, Deep Magenta, Cadmium Yellow Light, Phthalo Green, Ultramarine Blue)
artist's brushes (assorted sizes)

1. Fold the pillowcase into fourths and press the folds, using a warm iron. With the felt-tip marker, trace the design that you want to use, including the broken lines, on tracing paper. Slide the traced design inside the pillowcase and align the intersection of the broken lines with the intersection of the folds. Use the water-soluble pen to trace the design, excluding the broken lines, onto the pillowcase.

2. Mix the paint to desired colors. Using the pattern as a guide, paint the design. When the design is dry, outline it with contrasting colors of paint. Allow the paint to dry.

3. Rinse the pillowcase in cold water to remove the water-soluble pen markings. Wash, dry, and iron the pillowcase.

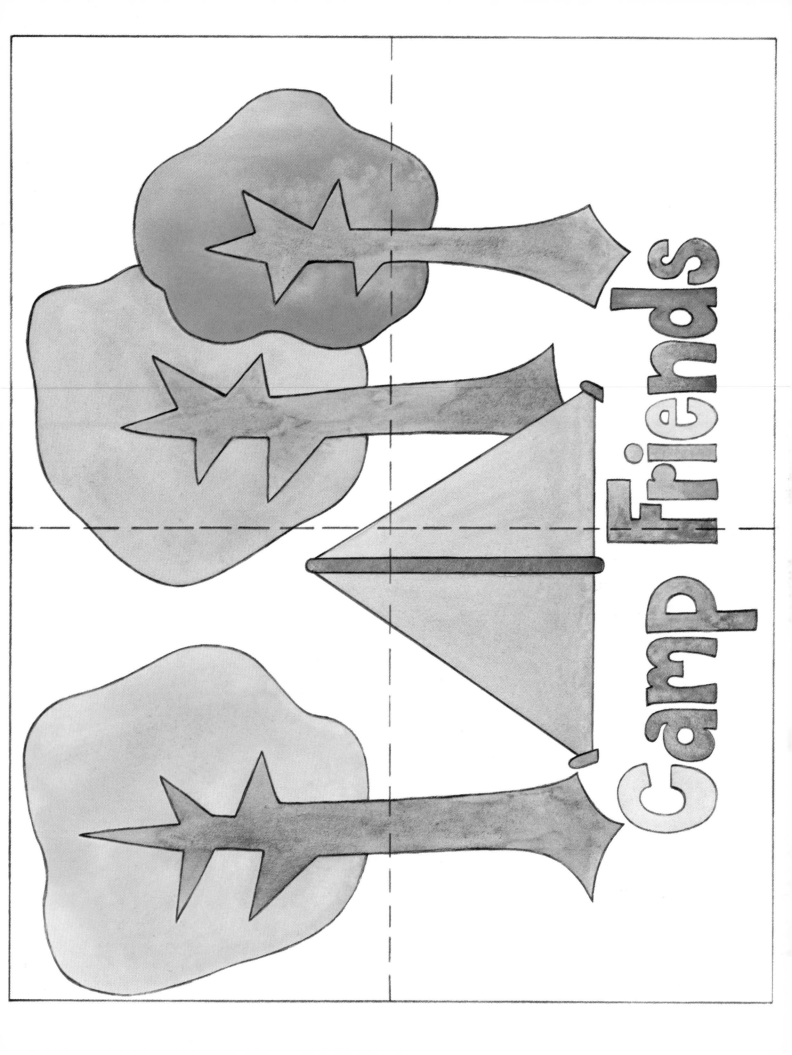

Camp Friends

The Sunday Bears

Say cheese, please . . . .
Papa, Mama, and Baby Bear
pose for the family portrait,
dressed in their Sunday best. Make
one or all of these gentle, woolen bears.
They'll capture any child's heart.

Making the Bears

You will need (for all three bears):
tape measure
1 yard (60″-wide) camel-colored wool
polyester stuffing
1 yard each black and rose embroidery
    floss
6 (⁷⁄₁₆″) black buttons (optional)
string (about 3 yards)
tapestry needle

1. Trace and cut out the patterns, adding ¼″ seam allowances. Pin the patterns to the wool fabric and cut. Transfer the markings for attaching the limbs.

2. Sew face front pieces, right sides together, at center front; press seams open. With right sides together, sew one side of forehead to one side of face front, stitching to center seam; sew other side. Trim point of triangle.

Embroider nose on face front, using satin stitch. Use straight stitch for sewing mouth. Sew on button eyes, or if bears are for a very young child, embroider the eyes. Satin-stitch the heart cheeks.

3. Sew ear pieces with right sides together, leaving bottom open. Clip the curves; turn ears right side out and press. Topstitch ½″ from the outer edge.

With raw edges aligned, sew ears to front of head, matching topstitching on ears with forehead seams. Sew back of head to front of head, right sides together, leaving neck open. Clip the curves and turn.

4. Sew body front pieces, right sides together; clip curve. Sew body front to back, leaving top open. Turn and stuff; slip-stitch opening closed.

5. Stuff head and turn raw edge under ¼″. Pin head to body, aligning center front seams, and sew together by hand.

6. With right sides together, sew pieces for arms and legs, leaving openings as marked. Turn limbs and stuff. Slip-stitch openings closed.

Position arms at side seams of each bear so that point of attachment is as follows: on Papa, 1¼″ below the neck seam; on Mama, 1″ below; and on Baby, ¾″ below. Position legs at side seams so point of attachment is as follows: on Papa, 5½″ below neck seam; on Mama, 4½″ below; on Baby, 3¾″ below.

Thread the tapestry needle with string. (Do not knot it.) Starting on the outside of one limb, push the needle through the limb, leaving a 4″ tail of string. Pull the needle back through the limb. (Figure A.) Tack the limb to the body twice, leaving another tail of string. (Figure B.) Tie a double knot with the strings and trim the ends. Repeat to attach other limbs.

Figure A

Figure B

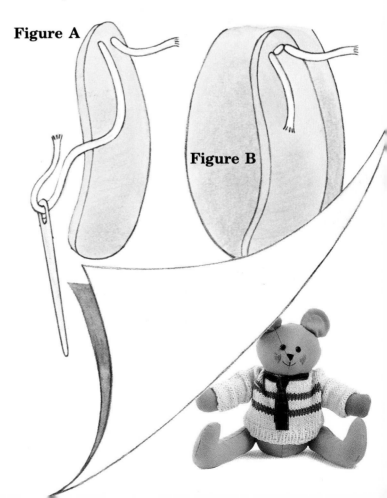

Making the Sweaters

You will need:
tapestry needle

For Papa: 1 skein natural 4-ply acrylic yarn (worsted weight), small amount green 4-ply acrylic yarn (worsted weight), #8 knitting needles, small strips of Velcro

For Mama: 1 skein pink 4-ply acrylic yarn (worsted weight), #8 knitting needles, ¾ yard (⅜″-wide) pink satin ribbon

For Baby: 1 skein blue 4-ply acrylic yarn (sport weight), #5 knitting needles, small strips of Velcro

Terms: sts (stitches), K (knit), P (purl), St st (stockinette stitch), beg (beginning), rep (repeat).
Gauge: for Papa and Mama, 4 sts = 1″; for Baby, 5 sts = 1″.

For Papa:
Front: Cast on 32 sts. K 1, P 1 for 5 rows. Change to St st and continue for 6 rows, ending with K row. At beg of 7th row, change to green yarn. Continue for 3 rows, ending with P row. Change to natural yarn. At beg of next row, cast on 16 sts for sleeve. K to end of row. Turn. Cast on 16 sts at beg of next row for other sleeve. Continue with natural for 4 rows.

On next row, *use natural for 16 sts, attach green for 32 sts, return to natural to finish row.* Rep between *s two more times. Continue in natural for 1½″. Bind off.
Left back: *Cast on 16 sts. K 1, P 1 for 5 rows. Change to St st and work even for 1¾″,* ending with K row. *At beg of next row, cast on 16 sts for sleeve. Continue in St st for 3″. Bind off.*
Right back: Rep between first two *s, ending with P row. Rep between last two *s.

For Mama:
Back: Cast on 30 sts. P first 2 rows. Change to St st and continue for 2½″, ending with P row. At beg of next row, cast on 14 sts for sleeve. K to end of row. Turn. Cast on 14 sts at beg of next row for other sleeve. Continue in St st for 2¼″; bind off.
Left front: *Cast on 15 sts. P first 2 rows. Continue in St st for 2½″*, ending with P row. *Cast on 14 sts for sleeve and K to end of row. Continue in St st for 2¼″; bind off.*
Right front: Rep between first two *s, ending with K row. Rep between last two *s.

For Baby:

Front: Cast on 24 sts. K 1, P 1 for 5 rows. Change to St st and continue for 1½", ending with P row. At beg of next row, cast on 10 sts for sleeve. K to end of row. Turn. At beg of next row, cast on 10 sts for other sleeve and P to end of row. Continue in St st for 2½". Bind off.

Left back: *Cast on 12 sts. K 1, P 1 for 5 rows. Change to St st, continue for 1½"*, ending with K row. *At beg of next row, cast on 10 sts for sleeve. Continue in St st for 2½". Bind off.*

Right back: Rep between first two *s, ending with P row. Rep between last two *s.

To Finish:

For each sweater, steam-press or block the pieces flat, being careful not to stretch them. Place the pieces with right sides together. Using the tapestry needle, whip-stitch the seams with matching yarn.

For Mama, thread the pink satin ribbon through the bound-off stitches on the sweater neck and tie a bow. For Papa and Baby, sew Velcro strips for fasteners onto the edges of the sweater backs.

Making the Accessories

You will need:

For Papa: ⅔ yard (1"-wide) taffeta plaid ribbon

For Mama: ½ yard (⅝"-wide) pink satin ribbon, tiny imitation flowers, white feather, white felt doll hat

For Baby: ¼ yard (½"-wide) white eyelet, ¼ yard (¾"-wide) black twill tape, scrap of camel-colored wool, polyester stuffing, black embroidery floss, 2 black seed beads (optional), ¼ yard (⅛"-wide) blue satin ribbon

1. For Papa, tie the plaid ribbon around his neck as you would a necktie. Trim the ends of the ribbon.

2. For Mama, tie the satin ribbon into a bow and slip the flowers and feather into the knot. Sew the bow to the crown of the hat. Place the hat on Mama's head and mark where the ears meet the hat. Cut slits in the hat and pull the ears through the slits.

3. For Baby, turn the ends of the eyelet under ¼", then ¼" again, and stitch. Put the eyelet around his neck and tack the ends together to make a collar. Make a loose knot in the center of the twill tape. Fold one end of the tape behind the other end so that the tape resembles a tie; tack it to the eyelet collar.

Transfer the pattern for Baby's bear to wool and cut out the pieces. Sew them with right sides together, leaving an opening. Turn the bear right side out and stuff lightly; sew opening closed. Embroider the nose and mouth; embroider the eyes or sew on bead eyes. Tie the ribbon around the bear's neck. Tack the bear to Baby's paw.

Add ¼″ seam allowances.

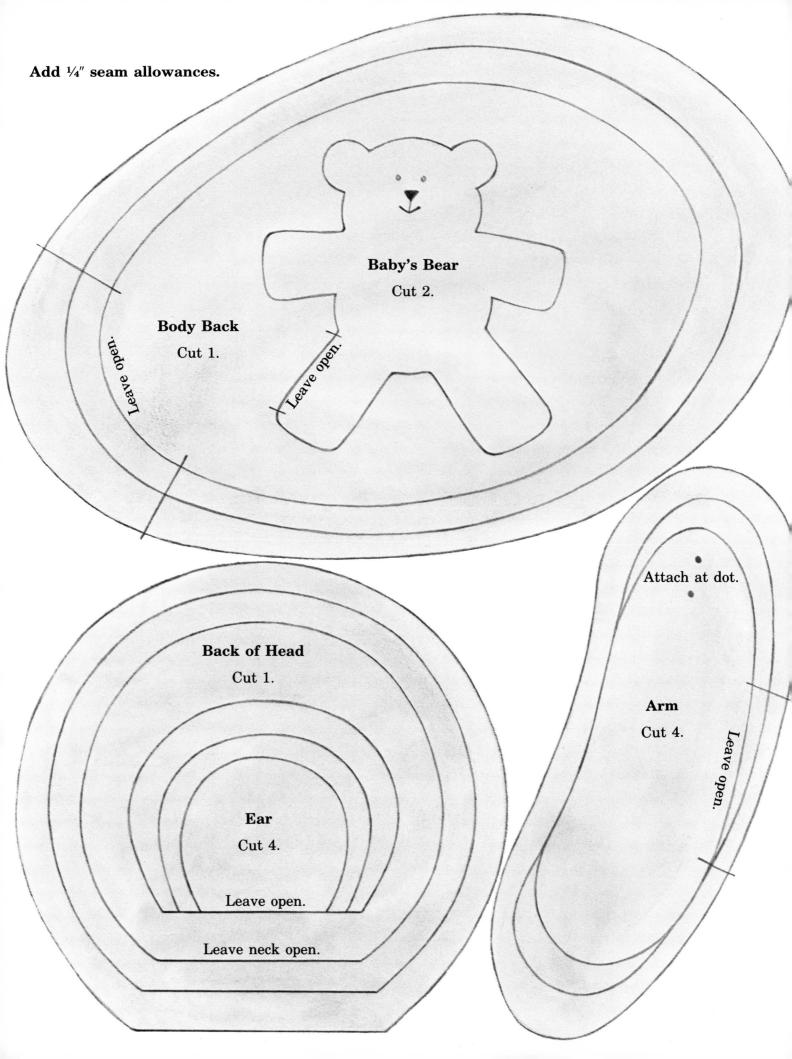

Baby's Bear

Cut 2.

Body Back

Cut 1.

Leave open.

Leave open.

Attach at dot.

Back of Head

Cut 1.

Arm

Cut 4.

Leave open.

Ear

Cut 4.

Leave open.

Leave neck open.

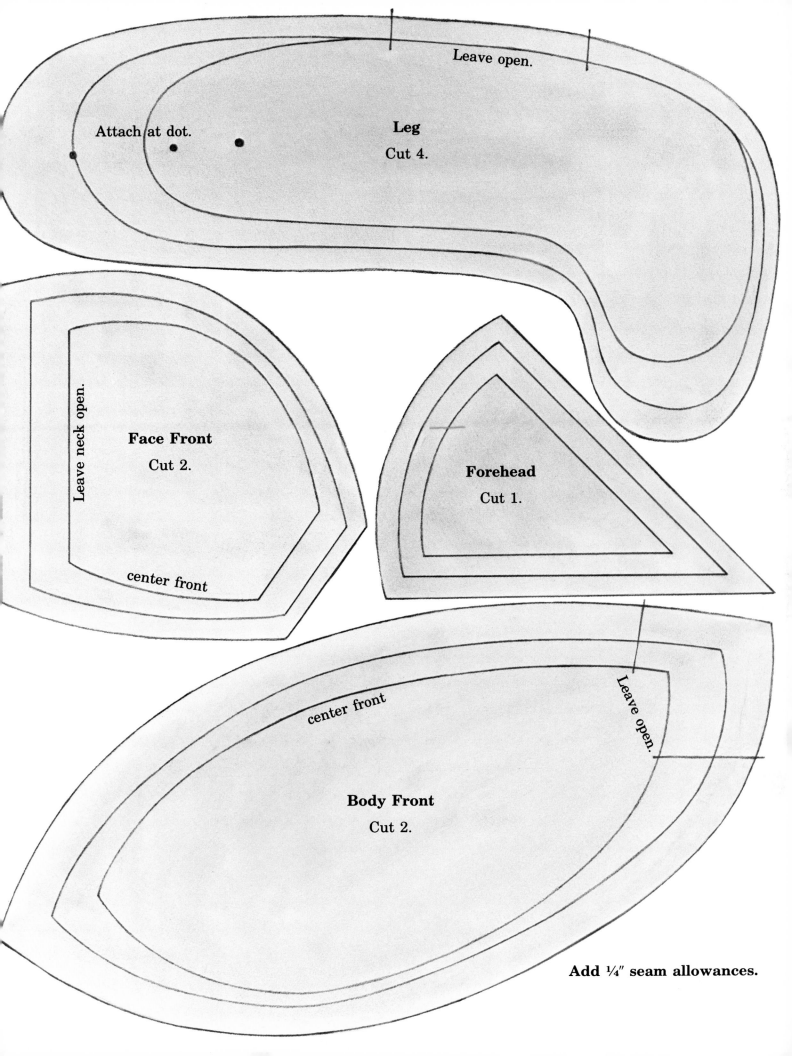

Leave open.

Attach at dot.

Leg

Cut 4.

Leave neck open.

Face Front

Cut 2.

center front

Forehead

Cut 1.

Leave open.

center front

Body Front

Cut 2.

Add ¼″ seam allowances.

A-to-Z Pocket Puppets

Tops on the list of great gifts for kids are these appealing, pocket-sized puppets, each waiting to be picked for its turn to teach or play. Whip up all twenty-six for a youngster who's eager to learn his ABCs, or fashion your favorites for stocking stuffers.

Pocket Puppets Keeper

You will need:
⅝ yard blue felt (at least 60″ wide)
yardstick
tailor's chalk
¼ yard red felt (at least 45″ wide)
1 package (1¼″-high) iron-on letters
2 (19″-long and ⅜″-diameter) wooden
  dowels
Tacky Glue
4 (2″) pom-poms
1½ yards (1″-wide) ribbon

1. Cut two 19″ x 29″ rectangles from the blue felt. Place one rectangle on top of the other.

2. On the top rectangle, chalk a line from side to side ½″ from the bottom edge. Starting 3½″ in from one side, mark off two 6″ sections on the line. (Figure A.)

Chalk another line from side to side 3½″ above the bottom edge of the rectangle. Starting ½″ in from one side, mark off three 6″ sections on the line. Using chalk, connect the upper and lower marks in a zigzag line. (Figure A.)

3. Sew along the zigzag line. Then sew together the remaining sides of the rectangles, using ½″ seam allowance and leaving a 5″ opening at the top for turning. Trim the fabric outside the zigzag line to ¼″; trim the points of the triangles. Trim the corners and turn the keeper right side out. Press, turning in the seam allowance at the opening. Slip-stitch the opening closed.

4. To make the pockets, cut five 2½″ x 19″ strips of red felt. Turning under the ends, pin the first strip so that the top edge is 3¾″ from the top edge of the keeper. Pin the other strips, spacing them 1½″ apart. Stitch the ends and the bot-

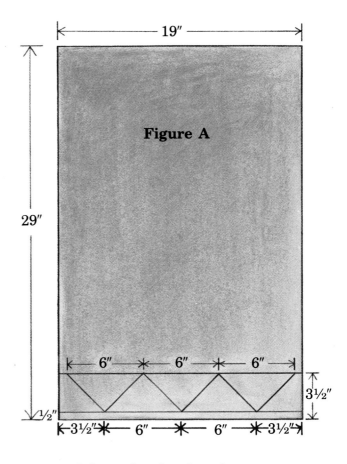

Figure A

toms of the strips, leaving the tops open. Using chalk, divide each strip into six 3″-wide sections. Stitch along the lines. Follow the directions on the package of iron-on letters to apply them to the pockets.

5. To make casings for the dowels, chalk lines from side to side 1″, 2¼″, 23½″, and 24¾″ from the top edge. Stitch along the lines. Clip side-seam stitching at casings and insert the dowels.

6. Glue pom-poms to the ends of the dowels. Glue the ends of the ribbon to the ends of the top dowel to form a hanger. When glue is dry, cut the ribbon in half and tie a bow with the ends.

Pocket Puppets

You will need:
felt in assorted colors
¼" wiggly-eyes (A,B,D,E,I,K,L,
  M,N,Q,V,W,X,Y,Z)
seed pearls (A,Q)
square of black or brown fur (B,W)
⅜" pom-poms (C,S)
black embroidery thread for eyes (C)
feathers (D,I)
⅛"-wide satin ribbon (F,H,J,X)
¼"-wide gold braid for trim (K,Q)
½"-wide gold braid for crowns (K,Q)
sequin (K)
black artificial flower stamens for
  whiskers (L,M,W)
black spoke sequins for eyelashes (M,P,Q)
6" pink chenille stem for tail (P)
½" pom-pom for tail (R)
⅛"-wide gold braid for trim (V)
hole punch
pinking shears (A,C,I,L)
Tacky Glue
permanent blue felt-tip marker (Y)

Note: Use the photographs as a guide for color selection and placement of trim pieces. Refer to above list and to patterns for additional information.

1. Trace and cut out the patterns. Cut out the felt pieces for each puppet, cutting two bodies and one face (if needed) as specified on the patterns.

2. For each puppet, position the felt pieces that are to be stitched between the body pieces. Machine-stitch the body pieces ⅛" from the edge, leaving openings as marked. Glue on the remaining felt pieces.

3. Use a hole punch to make felt circles for mouths (use half a circle for each) and eyes. Cut spoke sequins in half to form eyelashes. Trim the flower stamens to use for whiskers. Glue in place.

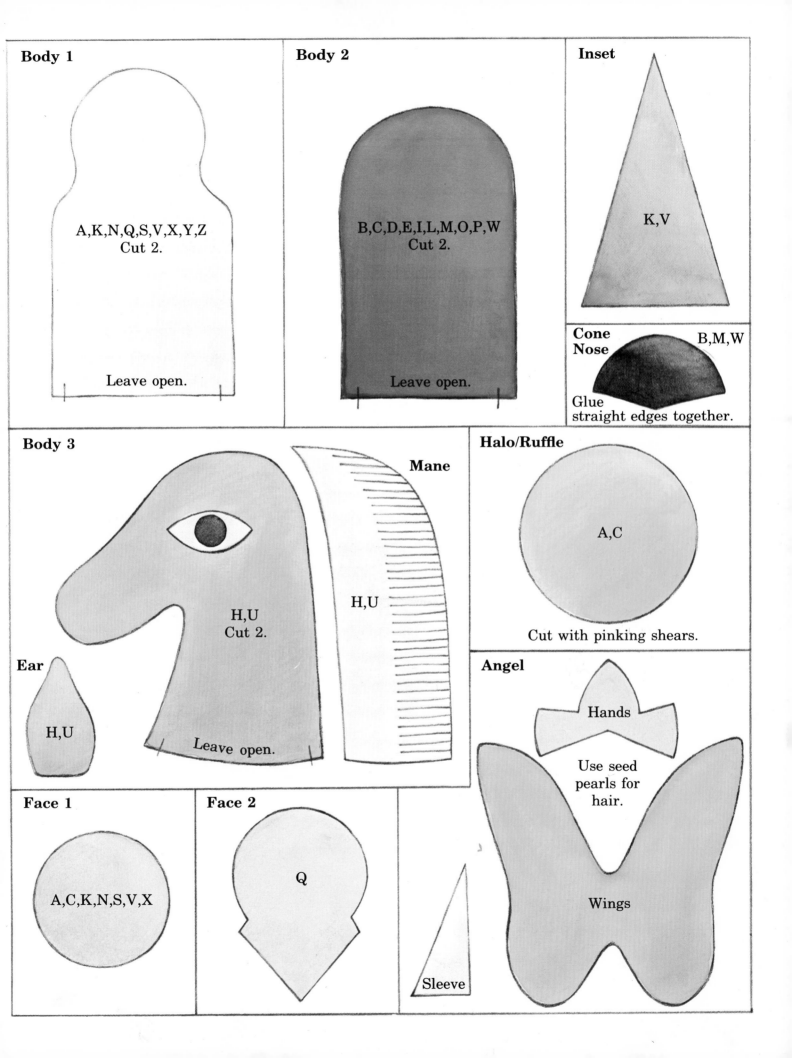

Body 1

A,K,N,Q,S,V,X,Y,Z
Cut 2.

Leave open.

Body 2

B,C,D,E,I,L,M,O,P,W
Cut 2.

Leave open.

Inset

K,V

**Cone
Nose**

B,M,W

Glue
straight edges together.

Body 3

Mane

H,U

H,U
Cut 2.

Leave open.

Ear

H,U

Halo/Ruffle

A,C

Cut with pinking shears.

Angel

Hands

Use seed
pearls for
hair.

Wings

Face 1

A,C,K,N,S,V,X

Face 2

Q

Sleeve

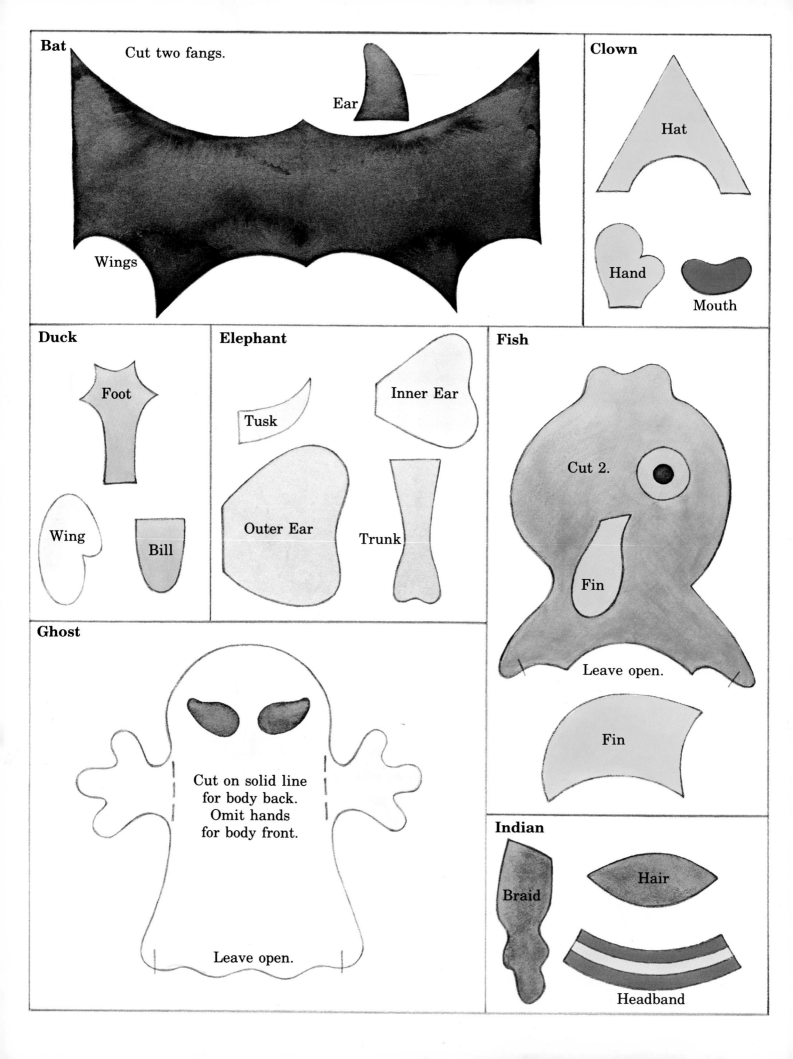

Bat

Cut two fangs.

Ear

Wings

Clown

Hat

Hand

Mouth

Duck

Foot

Wing

Bill

Elephant

Tusk

Inner Ear

Outer Ear

Trunk

Fish

Cut 2.

Fin

Leave open.

Fin

Ghost

Cut on solid line
for body back.
Omit hands
for body front.

Leave open.

Indian

Braid

Hair

Headband

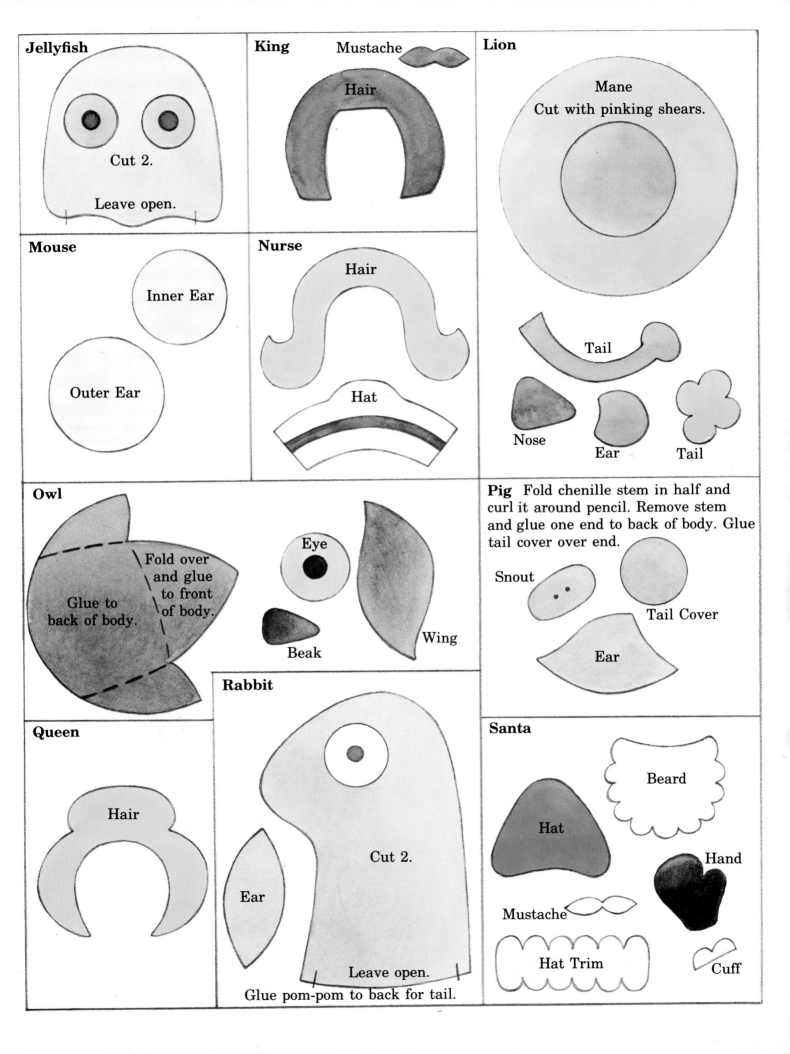

Jellyfish

Cut 2.

Leave open.

King

Mustache

Hair

Lion

Mane
Cut with pinking shears.

Mouse

Inner Ear

Outer Ear

Nurse

Hair

Hat

Tail

Nose

Ear

Tail

Owl

Glue to back of body.

Fold over and glue to front of body.

Eye

Beak

Wing

Pig Fold chenille stem in half and curl it around pencil. Remove stem and glue one end to back of body. Glue tail cover over end.

Snout

Tail Cover

Ear

Queen

Hair

Rabbit

Cut 2.

Ear

Leave open.
Glue pom-pom to back for tail.

Santa

Beard

Hat

Hand

Mustache

Hat Trim

Cuff

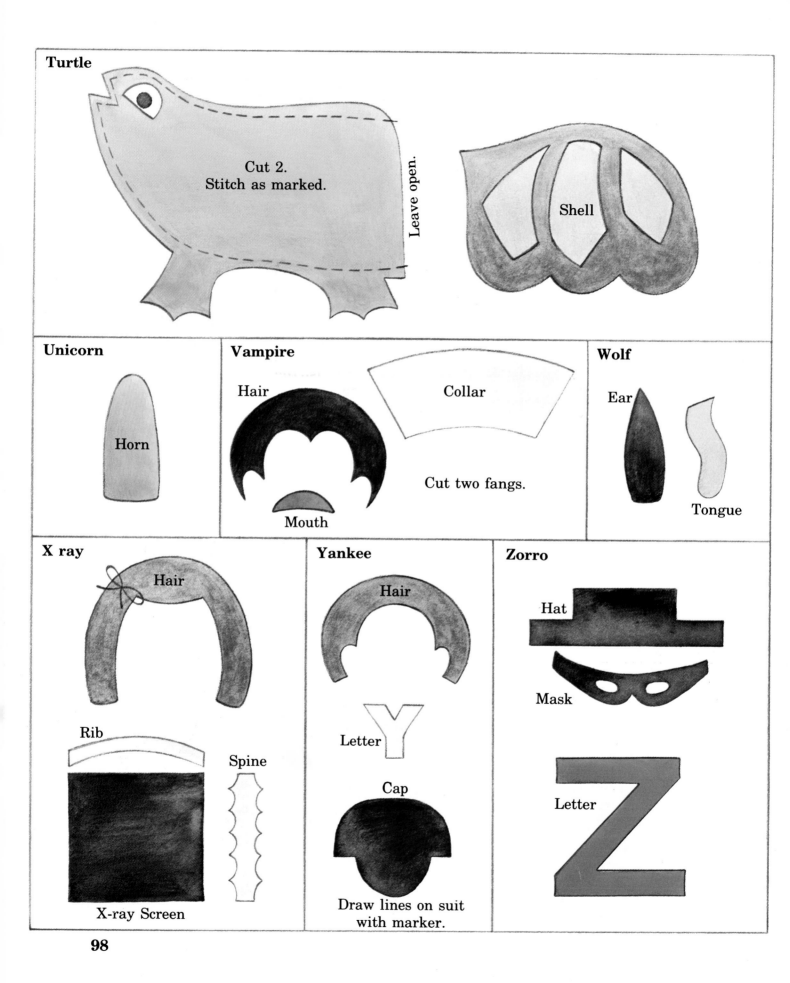

Turtle

Cut 2.
Stitch as marked.

Leave open.

Shell

Unicorn

Horn

Vampire

Hair

Collar

Cut two fangs.

Mouth

Wolf

Ear

Tongue

X ray

Hair

Rib

Spine

X-ray Screen

Yankee

Hair

Letter

Cap

Draw lines on suit
with marker.

Zorro

Hat

Mask

Letter

98

Something Fishy

This fish is a natural for toting towels and swimming togs to the pool or beach during the summer. The remainder of the year it can serve as a pajama bag—perfect for overnight trips to grandma's house.

The tote shown is made of kettle cloth, but if the rush is on and you need to make every minute count, choose a heavier fabric. Then you can forego the interfacing and lining, which are time-consuming and a bit tricky to attach. Do pink, zigzag, or clean-finish the seams if you do not line the tote.

99

You will need:
brown paper for pattern
¾ yard (45"-wide) yellow fabric
¾ yard (36"-wide) fleece-type interfacing
¾ yard (45"-wide) fabric for lining
16" yellow zipper
scraps of assorted print fabric
1 package (½"-wide) white bias tape
1 package (standard size) green rickrack
1 package (giant size) orange rickrack
scraps of solid white, blue, and green
   fabric
white embroidery floss
embroidery needle
tape measure
1 yard (⅞"-wide) yellow grosgrain ribbon
2 (1") D-rings
yellow embroidery floss

1. Enlarge the fish pattern to full size on brown paper, adding ½" seam allowance all around. Cut two fish each from the yellow fabric, interfacing, and lining.

On right sides of both yellow fish, transfer the four trim placement lines, three eye circles, and mouth line. On one right side, transfer placement marks for ribbon loops. Use this fish for the front.

On the top edges of the yellow fish, mark two dots for the zipper opening, using the 16" zipper as a measure. Mark dots for zipper openings on the interfacing and lining pieces, to match those on yellow fish. On lining pieces, mark trim line for tail.

2. From the print scraps, cut 34 pieces, each 3⅛" square. To form triangles for the fins, fold each square twice diagonally, and press.

On the yellow fish, use 12 triangles for side fins on the front and 12 for side fins on the back. Pin the raw edges of the triangles along the trim placement lines, overlapping the triangles with all double-fold edges facing in the same direction.

Zigzag-stitch along the lines, catching only the raw edges of the triangles.

Cover the zigzag stitching with strips of bias tape, topstitching along both edges; sew green rickrack along the edges of tape opposite the triangles. Sew two strips of bias tape, side by side, on the line nearest the eye; sew orange rickrack down the center.

Use the 10 remaining triangles for top and bottom fins. On the front fish, align the raw edges of the triangles with the raw edges of the fish (right sides together) and pin, overlapping the triangles with all double-fold edges facing in the same direction. Stitch.

3. Cut two 3" pieces of grosgrain ribbon. Slip a D-ring on each ribbon and fold the ribbon in half, cut ends together. On the front fish, align the ribbon ends with the raw edges as marked. Sew along the seam line.

4. Trace the patterns for the eye circles, adding ¼" seam allowances. From the white, blue, and green scraps, cut two circles each, as indicated. From the interfacing, cut two circles for each size eye circle, omitting the seam allowances.

Center and then pin the interfacing circles under the corresponding fabric circles. Turn under the seam allowances and press; clip curve to seamline. Pin the eyes to fish as marked and appliqué with slip stitch. Using white floss, make large French knots on the green circles; then embroider a mouth with stem stitch.

5. Pin interfacings to wrong sides of yellow front and back. Stitch the top seam from tail to back zipper dot and from front zipper dot to mouth, leaving an opening between the dots. Lay open the front and back with wrong sides up. Pin the zipper tape, with the zipper closed and face down, to the seam allowances only (do not pin to fish itself). Stitch. Open the zipper.

6. Trim away the tail on the lining pieces as marked on the pattern. Sew the pieces with right sides together, leaving zipper opening between dots in the top seam and a 4″ opening for turning in the bottom seam. Do not turn.

7. Align zipper opening of lining with zipper opening of tote. Pin seam allowance of one side of lining to seam allowance of one side of tote, right sides together and raw edges aligned. Sew, stitching through the two seam allowances and zipper tape only. Repeat for other side. Then sew around remainder of tote (mouth, bottom, and tail).

8. Turn tote right side out through opening in bottom of lining; slip-stitch opening closed. Smooth lining inside tote.

9. To finish, cut the remaining ribbon 3″ longer than the length desired for the shoulder strap. Turn under the ribbon ends ½″ and stitch. Slip the ends through the D-rings and fold to make 1″ loops. Sew across the loop ends twice, making the rows ¼″ apart.

For the tassel pull, cut six 10″ pieces of yellow floss. Pull the floss through the hole in the zipper tab. Even the ends and tie a knot.

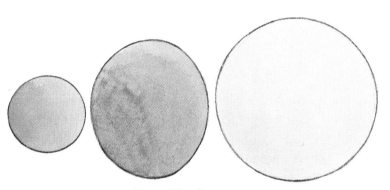

Eye Circles
Add ¼″ seam allowances.

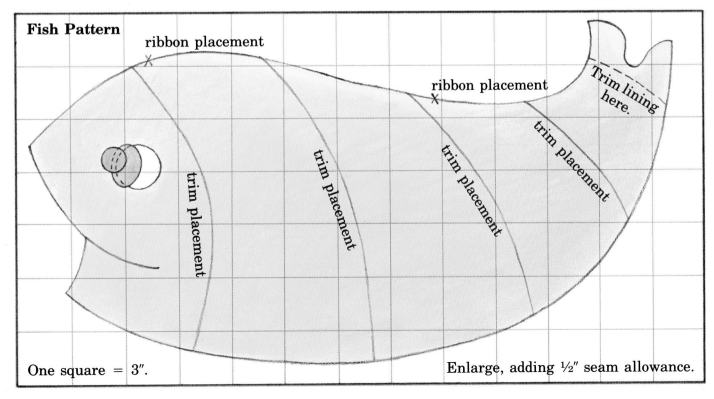

Fish Pattern

ribbon placement

ribbon placement

Trim lining here.

trim placement

trim placement

trim placement

trim placement

One square = 3″.

Enlarge, adding ½″ seam allowance.

Critter Box

Finding bugs and beetles is a favorite pastime of most little boys and many little girls. And for keeping the creatures that they catch, this cage will be a welcome replacement for jelly jars and cardboard boxes. The screening does double duty—allowing plenty of light and fresh air inside, while enabling youngsters to watch as the occupant creeps, jumps, or otherwise moves about. There's ample space, so a critter shouldn't mind his stay, as long as it's temporary and he's treated with kindness.

You will need:
1 (2′) 1 x 6
scroll saw (or jigsaw)
router and ¼″ straight blade
ruler or T square
7½″ x 20″ (¼″) plywood
sandpaper
walnut stain and brush
2½″ (1″-wide) hinge
1″ brads
10″ x 24″ piece of aluminum screening
10″ x 24″ piece of hardware cloth
staple gun and 5⁄16″ staples
9½″ piece of heavy-duty coathanger wire
paint and artist's brush

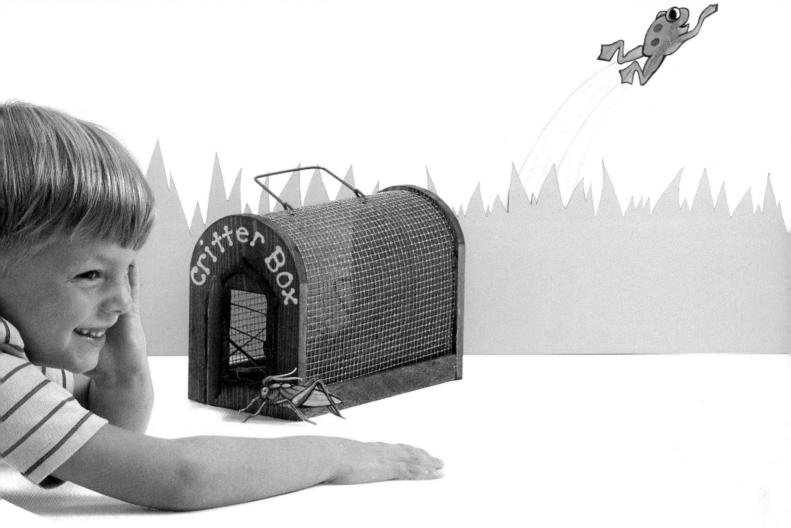

1. Transfer pattern for end panels to the 1 x 6, marking the door opening on front panel only. Using the scroll saw, cut out the panels; cut the door opening. On the back of each panel, rout ¼″ completely around the edges.

2. From the plywood, cut a 4⅞″ x 10″ panel for the bottom and two 1″ x 10″ strips for the sides. Transfer the patterns for the door frame, door, and latch to the plywood. Cut out the pieces. Cut the door away from the frame.

3. Sand and stain wood pieces. Let dry.

4. Attach the door to the door frame with the hinge. Use brads to tack the latch to the door frame and to tack the door frame to the front panel (over the door opening). Tack the bottom panel securely to the routed edges of the end panels.

5. Stretch screening over end panels along the routed edges and secure corners with brads. Place the hardware cloth over the screening and staple both layers to the routed edges. Tack the side strips to the box, covering the raw edges of the screening and hardware cloth.

6. Bend the wire to make a handle. Push the ends of the wire through the hardware cloth and bend them to secure the handle.

7. Paint "Critter Box" above the door. Let dry.

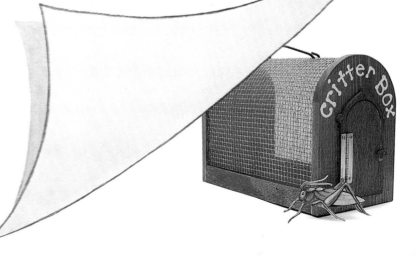

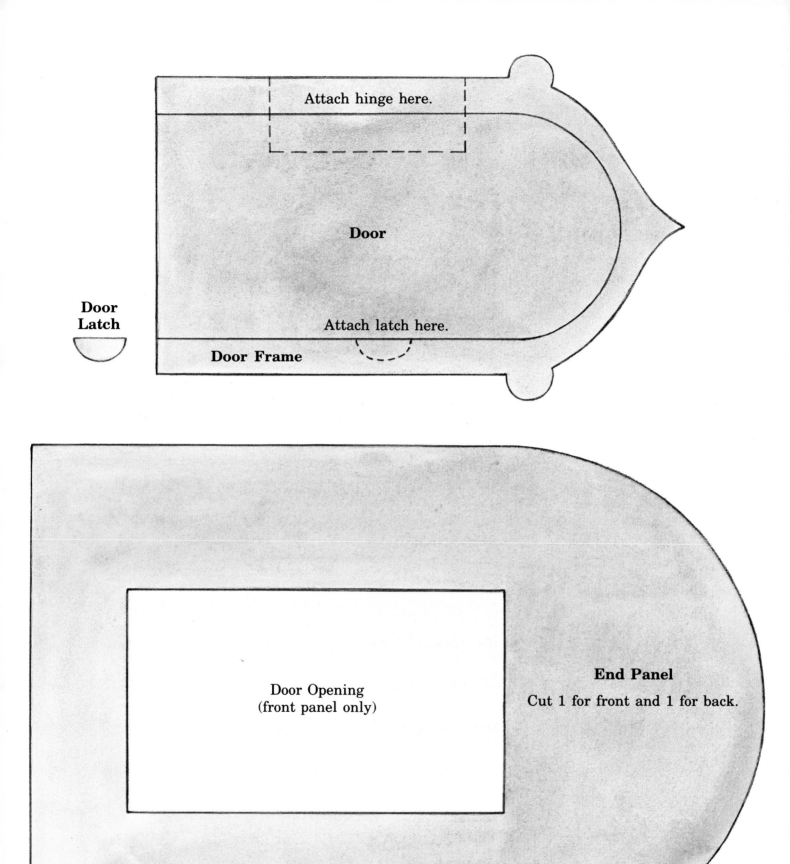

Attach hinge here.

Door

**Door
Latch**

Attach latch here.

Door Frame

Door Opening
(front panel only)

End Panel

Cut 1 for front and 1 for back.

104

Cookie Man Game

Looking for a last-minute gift for young nieces and nephews or the children who live next door? Here's a cute-as-a-button game that's suitable for both girls and boys. A tossing game, it consists of six felt cookie men and a cracker tin, turned cookie jar.

To play the game, each participant chooses three cookie men, either chocolate or butterscotch. The players then take turns standing behind a line and tossing the cookie men into the cookie jar, which has been placed several feet away. Each time a cookie man lands inside the jar, the player who made the toss scores a point. Whoever scores five points first, wins the game. (When scoring points becomes too easy, it's time to move the cookie jar farther from the line.)

You will need:
6 (9″ x 10½″) pieces of brown felt
6 (9″ x 10½″) pieces of gold felt
embroidery thread and needle
buttons for eyes and trim
white glue
plastic wiggly-eyes
rickrack, ribbon, lace, and other trim
heavy-duty thread
dried beans for stuffing
metal can (about 8½″ high x 7″ across)
   with lid
white enamel spray paint
alphabet stencil
red acrylic paint
paintbrush
2″ wooden knob for lid (optional)
#12 (⅜″ to ½″) sheet-metal screw
   (optional)

1. Trace and cut out the pattern for the cookie man. Cut six each from brown and gold felt.

2. On the fronts, use embroidery thread to chain-stitch the mouth. Satin-stitch the nose, by hand or machine. Sew on buttons for eyes, or glue on wiggly-eyes. Sew on the rickrack and other trim.

3. Pin the fronts to the backs, right sides together. Using heavy-duty thread and a short stitch, machine-stitch with ¼″ seam allowance, leaving openings for turning; stitch again to reinforce the seams. Clip the curves and turn.

4. Use the eraser end of a pencil to push out the curves. Fill the cookie men with beans (cookie men should be somewhat floppy) and sew the openings closed.

5. Spray the metal can with the white enamel paint and let dry. Using a pencil and the alphabet stencil, draw the letters on the can. Paint the letters and the wooden knob red. Allow to dry. Make a hole in the lid and attach the knob with the screw. Gently stuff the cookie men into the can.

Note: This is not a suitable gift for very young children because of the buttons, plastic eyes, and beans—any of which could be swallowed.

Cookie Man

Cut 6 brown and 6 gold.

Leave open.

Just Clowning Around

Let the good times roll! Loaded with personality, these lively clowns are always ready for play.

Note that the instructions are for making the fluffy-haired clown in the yellow suit, at right. You'll find directions for making his fuzzy-haired chums, below, in the list of variations.

You will need (for the clown in the yellow suit):

⅔ yard (45″-wide) print fabric for suit and hat
¼ yard (36″-wide) solid fabric for ruffle
scraps of felt in white, red, and black
twine
4 (1″) pom-poms for suit and hat
rickrack
red embroidery floss
polyester stuffing
1 (3″) plastic foam ball
white cotton ankle sock (size 9½)
curved needle for attaching hair
white paint for eyes
1 (¾″) pom-pom for nose
30″ piece of heavy wire
2″ x 5″ piece of cardboard
1 skein of 2-ply knitting yarn
heavy-duty sewing thread

1. Cut the suit, hat, and a 6″ x 36″ strip for the ruffle from selected fabrics. Cut the shoe tops and hands from white felt and the shoe soles from red felt. Use ¼″ seam allowance throughout unless instructed otherwise.

2. To make the suit, place the two pieces with right sides together and stitch one shoulder. Turn the neck edge under ½″ and stitch to make a casing. Stitch the other shoulder seam to within ½″ of casing. Run twine through the casing for a drawstring.

To hem the sleeves and legs, turn under the edges ⅛″, then ⅛″ again, and machine-stitch. Sew the underarm and side seams on each side of the suit. Stitch the inside seam of the legs.

Clip the seams at the curves. Turn and press. Sew three pom-poms to the front of the suit as marked on the pattern.

3. For the ruffle, fold the strip lengthwise with right sides together and sew the long edge. Turn right side out and sew a seam ½″ from first seam to form a casing. Thread twine through the casing for a drawstring.

Trim the outer edge of the ruffle with rickrack. Join the ends of the ruffle with a French seam, leaving the casing free.

4. With a running stitch and three strands of embroidery floss, sew together the two pieces for each hand (⅛″ seam allowance), leaving the wrist edge open for stuffing. Do not turn.

Sew tucks on the shoe tops as marked on pattern. With wrong sides together,

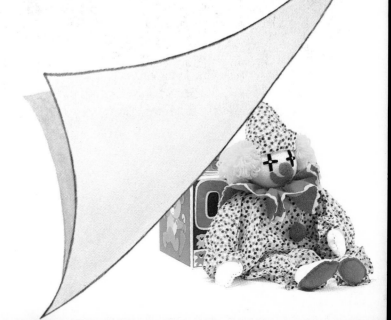

use a running stitch and embroidery floss to sew the back seam of each shoe top, stitching only to the X as marked on pattern (⅛" seam allowance). Align soles with shoe tops and sew with a running stitch (⅛" seam allowance). Do not turn.

Stuff the hands and feet with polyester stuffing and tack the openings closed. Place the hands with thumbs up inside the suit sleeves. Wrap a piece of twine 1½" from the edge of each sleeve, wrapping the twine tightly to secure the hand and to make a ruffle. Tie and knot the twine. Secure the feet inside the suit legs in the same manner.

5. Place the plastic foam ball in the toe of the sock and tightly tie a piece of twine beneath the ball. Stuff the sock to within 1" of opening with polyester stuffing. Tie off the opening.

Place the sock inside the suit, aligning the "neck" of the sock with the neck of the suit. Pull the drawstring and knot it. Place the ruffle around the neck. Tighten and then secure the drawstring.

6. To make the hat, stitch together the straight edges of one piece with right sides together (⅛" seam allowance). Turn right side out. For the lining, stitch the second piece same as first, but leave a 2" opening for turning as marked on pattern. Do not turn.

Aligning seams, place the hat inside the lining (right sides will be facing) and stitch together the edges of the brim. Turn hat through opening in lining. Whipstitch opening closed.

Position lining inside hat and press. Tack a pom-pom to the tip of the hat.

7. Lightly stuff the bottom half of the hat. With the seam at the back and the brim down, place the hat on the head so

that the hat is tilted toward the back.

Using a curved needle and doubled thread, sew the hat to the head 1¼" from the edge of the brim; turn up the brim. Pull down the top of the hat to one side and tack lightly at the fold to secure the stuffing.

8. Cut the mouth from red felt and two strips for each eye from black felt and glue them in place. Paint the centers of the eyes white. Tack a pom-pom for the nose above the mouth.

9. To make the hair, bend the heavy wire, punch holes in the cardboard, and assemble the wire and cardboard as shown. (Figure A.)

Wrap knitting yarn around the wire about forty times. Machine-stitch down the center of the yarn. (Figure B.) Remove the yarn and tie a piece of twine around it, over the machine stitching. Pull the twine tightly to make a pom-pom. Knot the twine and cut the ends.

Make six more pom-poms. Using heavy-duty thread, sew the pom-poms to the clown's head, beneath the hat brim.

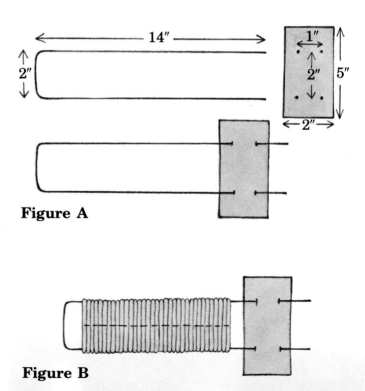

Figure A

Figure B

Variations

• Make two ruffles, using a 6″ x 36″ strip of print fabric for the first and a 3¾″ x 35″ strip of solid fabric for the second. Follow Step 3 to sew and attach the ruffles.

• Tack a pom-pom to each shoe top.

• For a hat that does not flop, stuff the entire hat instead of just the bottom.

• Make the eyes a different shape.

• To make a clown with fuzzy hair, you will need about three yards of twisted macrame cord (6mm). Follow Step 1 through Step 6. Then assemble the wire and cardboard as instructed in Step 9.
   Wrap the macrame cord around the wire. Machine-stitch across the top of the cord, just beneath the wire. Remove the cord from the wire and cut the loops opposite the line of stitching. (Figure C.) Machine-stitch the hair, along the line of stitching, to the inside of the hat 1½″ from the brim edge.
   Stuff the hat and place it on the clown's head, tilting the hat toward the back. Using a curved needle and doubled thread, sew the hat to the head. Turn up the brim. Comb and trim the hair. Follow Step 8 to complete the clown.

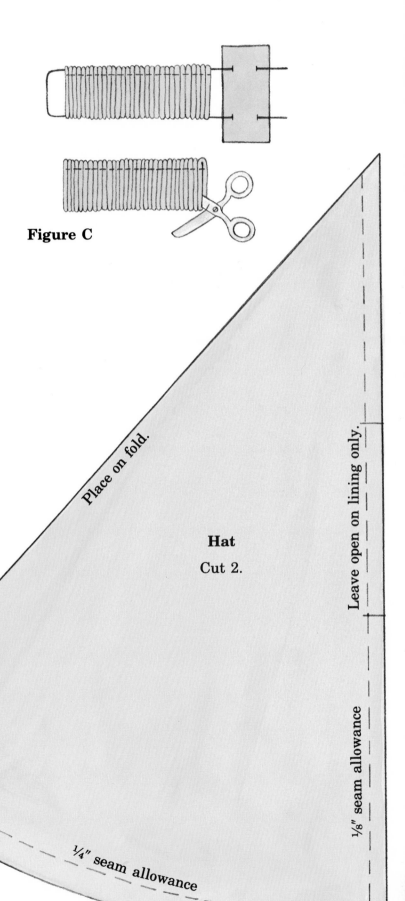

Figure C

Place on fold.

Hat

Cut 2.

Leave open on lining only.

¼″ seam allowance

⅛″ seam allowance

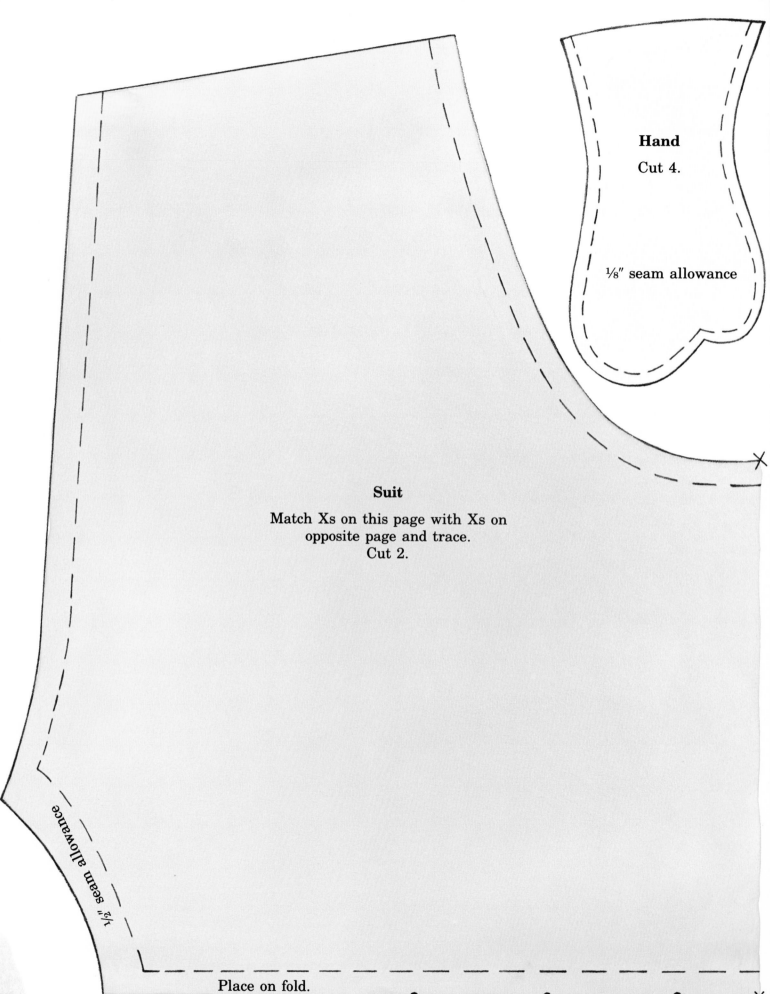

Hand

Cut 4.

⅛″ seam allowance

Suit

Match Xs on this page with Xs on
opposite page and trace.
Cut 2.

½″ seam allowance

Place on fold.

pom-pom placement

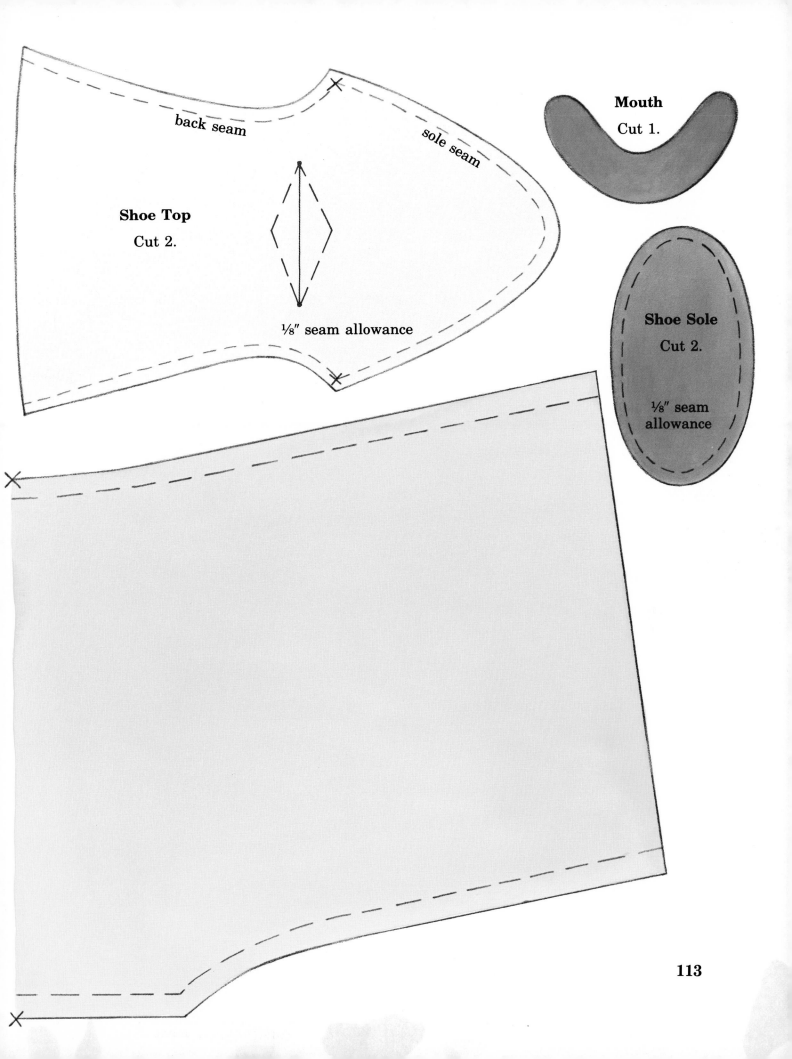

Mouth

Cut 1.

Shoe Top

Cut 2.

⅛″ seam allowance

back seam

sole seam

Shoe Sole

Cut 2.

⅛″ seam
allowance

113

Kiddie Car

Parked amid toys or in front of the TV, this plump pillow is comfy to sit or lean on, or to rest a tired little head on. Bright red poplin gives the rounded body a sporty look, but it's the wobbly wheels, shiny lamé bumpers, and friendly smile that put this car in a class all its own—downright lovable!

You will need:
brown paper for pattern
tape measure
1½ yards (45"-wide) red poplin
⅛ yard (45"-wide) white poplin
scraps of felt in red, blue, and white
¼ yard (72"-wide) black felt
sewing thread to match colors of fabrics
2" square of interfacing
9 (1 lb.) bags polyester stuffing
white glue
⅛ yard (60"-wide) silver lamé

4 (1") silver shank buttons
6 large snaps
2 small snaps
5½" x 8" piece of fabric for license plate
3½" x 5" piece of poster paper

Note: For more uniform stitches, slightly loosen top tension on your sewing machine when using satin stitch. Use ¼" seam allowance for sewing the car.

1. Enlarge pattern for side of car, adding ¼" seam allowance. Cut two from red fabric and transfer markings. From same fabric, cut two 13" strips across the width.

Enlarge patterns for side windows (front and back) and cut two each from white fabric. Trace the pattern for the front and rear windows; cut two (one front and one rear) from white fabric.

Trace patterns for nose, eyes, and corners of mouth and cut from felt. For mouth, cut a 7½" x ¼" strip from red felt.

2. Position the four side windows on car sides. Using satin stitch, sew around the windows, leaving a 3" opening on each front side window as marked on pattern.

On front side windows, position whites of eyes and satin-stitch along the back edges, leaving the front edges open as marked. Place an iris over each white and satin-stitch completely around iris, beginning at lower corner.

Cut four 1" squares of interfacing. On wrong side of car sides, center squares over marks for wheel placement and pin. Stitch along edges of squares.

3. With right sides together, sew two short ends of the 13" x 45" red strips to make one long strip; press seam open. Measure 17¼" from one end of strip and center bottom edge of front window; pin window in place. Center and pin top edge of rear window 32½" from same end of strip. Sew windows to strip, using satin stitch.

Beginning ¼" from end of strip and at notch on car side, sew one long edge of strip to one car side, stitching in direction of arrow and clipping curves as you sew; repeat for other side. Trim excess fabric at end of strip, leaving ¼" seam allowance for closing.

Turn car right side out and stuff firmly. Slip-stitch opening closed.

4. Glue eyelashes, pupils, mouth, and mouth corners to car. Sew dart on nose and slip-stitch in place, stuffing lightly as you sew.

5. For the tires, cut eight 7½" circles from black felt. Transfer pattern for hubcaps to silver lamé and cut four.

Sew together two circles of felt for each tire, stitching around outer edge and leaving a 3" opening for turning. Turn tires right side out and pin hubcaps to center. Satin-stitch around outer edge of hubcaps. In center of hubcaps, mark buttonholes; sew and slit.

Stuff tires and slip-stitch openings closed. Sew buttons to car as marked; attach tires to the car.

6. For the bumpers, cut four 2½" x 18½" strips of lamé and round off the corners. With right sides together, sew along edges of two strips for each bumper, leaving an opening in one long end of each for turning. Turn bumpers and stuff lightly; slip-stitch opening closed. Use large snaps to attach bumpers to car.

7. For the license plate, cut fabric in half crosswise. Print desired name on right side of one piece. Satin-stitch the letters, using contrasting thread.

Sew the two pieces with right sides together, leaving one end open. Turn. Slide poster paper through opening; slip-stitch opening closed. Attach license plate to car with small snaps.

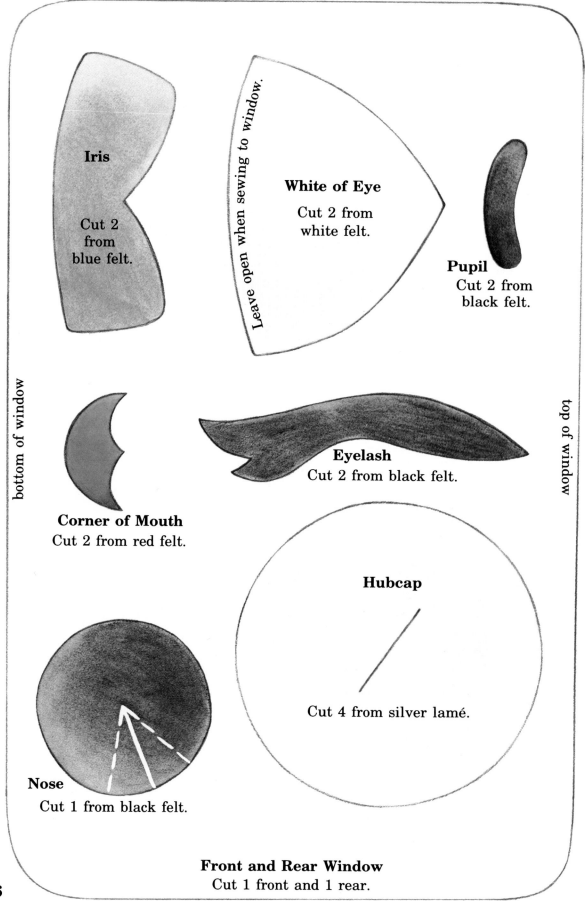

Iris

Cut 2 from blue felt.

Leave open when sewing to window.

White of Eye

Cut 2 from white felt.

Pupil

Cut 2 from black felt.

bottom of window

top of window

Corner of Mouth

Cut 2 from red felt.

Eyelash

Cut 2 from black felt.

Hubcap

Cut 4 from silver lamé.

Nose

Cut 1 from black felt.

Front and Rear Window

Cut 1 front and 1 rear.

116

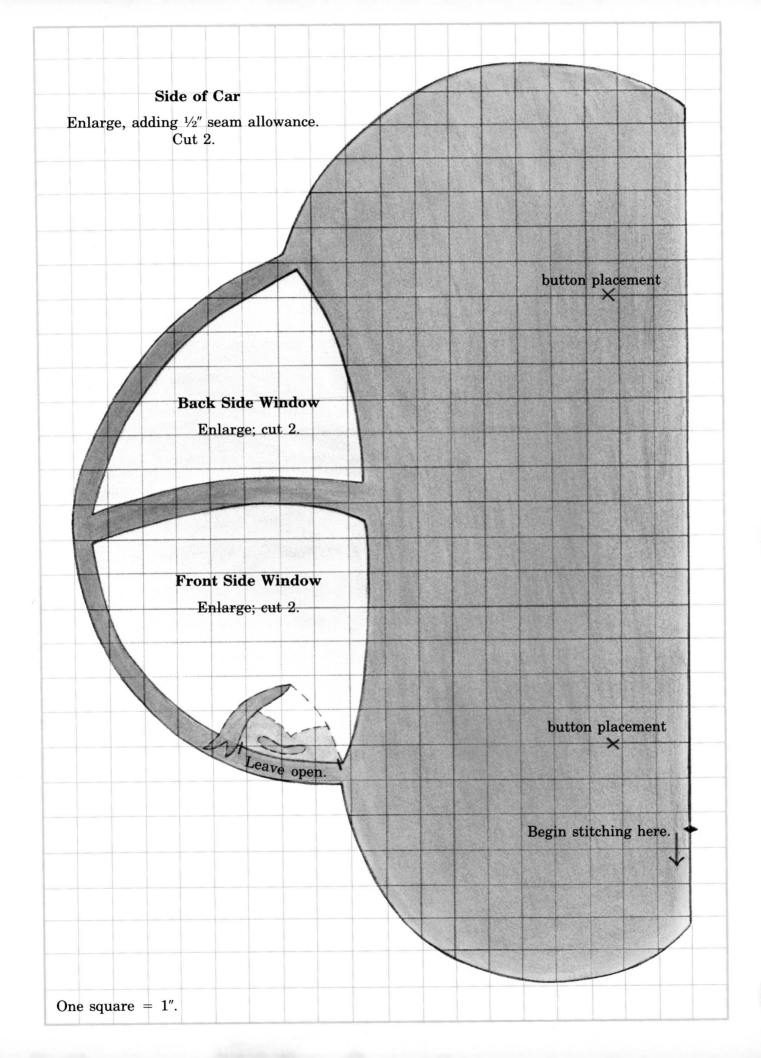

Side of Car

Enlarge, adding ½″ seam allowance.
Cut 2.

button placement
✕

Back Side Window

Enlarge; cut 2.

Front Side Window

Enlarge; cut 2.

button placement
✕

Leave open.

Begin stitching here.

One square = 1″.

Ducky Doodle

Howdy do, Ducky Doodle! Made of plywood, this chalkboard is lightweight and just the right size for little laps. As handsome as he is charming, Ducky Doodle will be decorative as well as entertaining.

You will need:
brown paper for pattern
carbon paper
12½" x 18½" (¼") plywood
scroll saw
drill with ¼" drill bit
1 sheet each of 180 and 220 grit
   sandpaper
acrylic paint (white, yellow, red, and
   black)
paintbrushes (¾" flat and #3 round)
1 pint blackboard slating
sponge brush
paper towels
5" x 27" strip of fabric for bow

1. Enlarge pattern for duck to full size. Using carbon paper and pencil, transfer outline of duck, including opening between feet, onto wood.

2. Cut out duck with scroll saw. Drill a hole in opening between feet. Thread scroll saw blade through hole and cut opening. Sand front, back, and edges of duck with 180 grit sandpaper, sanding with the grain; repeat, using 220 grit sandpaper.

3. Paint all surfaces with white acrylic paint, using ¾" flat brush; let dry. Apply three more coats, allowing paint to dry after each application. Use carbon paper to transfer features onto front of duck.

4. Using sponge brush, paint tummy with slating; let dry according to instructions on can. Sand slating lightly with 220 grit sandpaper and then wipe with moist paper towel. Repeat entire procedure three times.

5. For orange paint, mix yellow and red. Paint feet and bill with four coats, using #3 brush and letting paint dry after each application. Paint the eyes and nostrils black.

6. For the bow, fold the fabric strip in half lengthwise with right sides together. Sew across ends at an angle. Sew long edges opposite fold, using ¼" seam allowance and leaving a 2" opening in the middle. Trim corner seams and turn; slipstitch opening closed. Tie the bow around the duck's neck.

Note: To prime the chalkboard, turn a piece of chalk on its side and apply evenly. Erase with a damp sponge.

One square = 1″.

DESIGNERS & CONTRIBUTORS

Peyton Carmichael, Super Surprise Balls, 54; Art Easel, 72; Dolly's Closet, 76.

Karen C. Clenney, On Your Mark, 52.

Carolyn Vosburg Hall, Cookie Man Game, 105.

Linda Hendrickson, Tub-Time Toys, 44; Friendship Pillowcases, 82; Ducky Doodle, 118.

Zuelia Ann Hurt, "Sew-Easy" Christmas Cards, 36; Something Fishy, 99.

Butch Krutchik, Paper Sack House Wrap, ©1983 Bagriculture™, 34.

Pam Melton, These Are Tops, 18; Critter Box, 102.

P J's (Judy Childs, Sharon Cuppett, Peggy Musgrove), Tacky Tops, 60.

Dot Renneker, Sweet Street, 28.

Vasha Rosenblum, Quickie Quackers, 40; A-to-Z Pocket Puppets, 92.

Walter M. Rush, Jr., construction of Art Easel, 72, and Dolly's Closet, 76.

Robin D. Snyder, Sailboat Desk Set, 46.

Linda Martin Stewart, Just Ducky, 6; Snappy Soapbox Shopping Bags, 8.

Kathleen A. Taylor, Here We Go Loop-De-Loop, 27; Tidings from Teddy, 32; Kooky Caps, 61; Froggy Backpack, 66; The Sunday Bears, 86.

Dian Thomas, Candy Cane Reindeer, 10.

Carol Tipton, Away in a Manger, 22.

Barbara Whaley, Just Clowning Around, 108.

Madeline O'Brien White, Rainbow Lollipops, 4; Take-the-Cake Cupcakes, 12; Pop-Silly-Sicles, 15; Sweet Street, 28; Perky Paper Reindeer Wrap, 30; Cookie Creations, 43; Art Apron and Box, 72.

Judy Williams, Kiddie Car, 114.

Linda Baltzell Wright, A "Beary" Nice Candle Ring, 20; Color an Ice Candle, 50.

Dot Young, Cross-Stitched Choo-Choo, 64; Sailboat Sweater, 70.

Special thanks to the following enterprises in Birmingham, Alabama, for sharing their resources: Chocolate Soup, Inc.; Kiddieland; Playfair, Inc.; and Rich's, Inc.